APPLYING THE CONSTITUTION OF THE REPUBLIC OF POLAND IN HORIZONTAL RELATIONS

Monika Florczak-Wątor

APPLYING THE CONSTITUTION OF THE REPUBLIC OF POLAND IN HORIZONTAL RELATIONS

Jagiellonian University Press

The research for this publication was made possible by a grant from the Foundation for Polish Science (Fundacja na rzecz Nauki Polskiej) – POMOST BIS / 2012 – 6 / 2. Printing funded by the Department of Constitutional Law, Jagiellonian University

Translation
Joanna Miler-Cassino, Anna Setkowicz-Ryszka

Reviewer
Prof. Piotr Tuleja

Cover design
Andrzej Pilichowski-Ragno

ISBN 978-83-233-4017-1
ISBN 978-83-233-9319-1 (e-book)

JAGIELLONIAN
UNIVERSITY PRESS

www.wuj.pl

Jagiellonian University Press
Editorial Offices: Michałowskiego 9/2, 31-126 Kraków
Phone: +48 12 663 23 81, +48 12 663 23 82, Fax: +48 12 663 23 83
Distribution: Phone: +48 12 631 01 97, Fax: +48 12 631 01 98
Cell Phone: + 48 506006 674, e-mail: sprzedaz@wuj.pl
Bank: PEKAO SA, IBAN PL 80 1240 4722 1111 0000 4856 3325

CONTENTS

Introduction 7

1. The Problem of the Horizontal Effect of Constitutional Rights during
   the Drafting of the Polish Constitution.. 13
   1.1. The Period Preceding the Drafting of the Constitution 13
   1.2. Solutions Adopted in Drafts of the Constitution 15
   1.3. Discussion on the Inclusion of the Horizontal Effect Clause 17
   1.4. Conclusions Impacting the Interpretation of Constitutional Provisions....... 18

2. Holders of Constitutional Rights and Freedoms.. 21
   2.1. Regulation of Rights and Freedoms in the Polish Constitution 21
   2.2. The Principle of Universal Enjoyment of Constitutional Rights and
        Freedoms.. 24
   2.3. Citizen as a Holder of Constitutional Rights and Freedoms 25
   2.4. Special Definitions of Holders of Constitutional Rights and Freedoms........ 27
   2.5. Question of the Constitutional Personality of Entities Performing
        the Functions of Public Authorities.. 28
   2.6. Question of the Constitutional Personality of Public-Sector Economic
        Entities... 30

3. Direct Application of the Constitution as the Condition for the Horizontal
   Effect of Constitutional Rights and Freedoms 35
   3.1. Normative Content of the Principle of Direct Application of the
        Constitution... 35
   3.2. The Principle of Direct Application of the Constitution versus
        the Principle of its Supremacy.. 37
   3.3. Conditions Underlying the Direct Application of the Constitution............ 38
   3.4. Forms of Direct Application of the Constitution 40
        3.4.1. Autonomous Application of the Constitution 40
        3.4.2. Co-application of the Constitution and Statutes 44
        3.4.3. Control Application of the Constitution and Statutes 46
   3.5. Exceptions to the Rule of Direct Application of the Constitution 48

4. The Scope of the Horizontal Effect of Constitutional Rights 51
   4.1. Preliminary Remarks 51
   4.2. The Notion of Collision of Constitutional Rights 52
   4.3. Constitutional Rights as Principles (Optimization Requirements) 53
   4.4. The Principle of Proportionality and Its Importance for the Horizontal
        Effect of Constitutional Rights 55
   4.5. The Mechanism of Balancing Values Underlying Constitutional Rights....... 62
        4.5.1. The Notion of Values 62
        4.5.2. Axiological Foundations of the Constitution......................... 65
        4.5.3. Axiology of Constitutional Rights and Freedoms of an Individual........ 68
        4.5.4. Principles of the Value Balancing Mechanism 70

4.5.5. The Principle of Respecting Constitutional Rights and Freedoms as
a Natural Method of Resolving Collisions of Constitutional Rights 74
4.6. Closing Remarks 76

5. Adaptations of Models of the Horizontal Effect of Constitutional Rights and Free-
doms in the Polish Constitutional Reality 79
5.1. The Model of the Direct Horizontal Effect of Constitutional Rights 80
5.1.1. Preliminary Remarks 80
5.1.2. Characteristics of the Model Based on Examples of States Where it is
Applied 81
5.1.3. Rights and Freedoms in the Polish Constitution which are Capable
of Direct Horizontal Effect 86
5.1.4. Private Entities as Entities Beholden to Implement Constitutional
Rights and Freedoms 89
5.1.5. Obligations Correlated with Constitutional Rights and Freedoms 94
5.1.6. Consequences of Infringements of Constitutional Rights and
Freedoms by Private Entities 97
5.1.7. Closing Remarks 104
5.2. The Model of the Indirect Horizontal Effect of Constitutional Rights 105
5.2.1. Preliminary Remarks 105
5.2.2. Characteristics of the Model Based on Examples of States Where it
is Applied 106
5.2.3. Transposition of Constitutional Values into Private Law as a Result
of the Direct Application of the Polish Constitution 109
5.2.3.1. Basic Assumptions of the Constitutional Values Radiating
Effect 109
5.2.3.2. The Role of General Clauses and Other Indeterminate
Phrases 110
5.2.3.3. Co-Application of the Constitution and Statutes as a Method
of Endowing General Clauses and Other Indeterminate Phrases
with Contents 116
5.2.3.4. The Court as the Authority Transposing Constitutional Values
into Private Law 118
5.2.3.5. Controlling the Manner of Transposing Constitutional Values
into Private Law 119
5.2.3.6. Closing Remarks 122
5.3. The Model of the State's Protective Obligations in Horizontal Relations 122
5.3.1. Preliminary Remarks 122
5.3.2. Characteristics of the Model Based on Example of State Where it is
Applied 124
5.3.3. The State as an Entity Beholden to Implement Constitutional Rights
and Freedoms 126
5.3.4. Positive Character of the State's Obligation to Protect Constitutional
Rights and Freedoms of Individuals 128
5.3.5. Obligation for the State to Protect the Weaker Party to the Horizontal
Relation 132
5.3.6. Closing Remarks 136

Conclusion 139

Bibliography 143

INTRODUCTION

There is no doubt in contemporary jurisprudence that constitutional norms, including those that enshrine rights and freedoms, not only determine the shape of the relations between an individual and the state (so-called vertical relations), but also influence relations between private entities (so-called horizontal relations). This is so, because private law may not be formed independently of the constitution, which has the supreme legal force,[1] while relations between private entities may not be entirely detached from the rights guaranteed by the state to the parties to these relations.[2] In view of the foregoing, for several decades now, in the legal literature of a number of countries references have been made to the horizontal application of constitutional rights, their horizontal dimension or their horizontal effect.

The need to take constitutional rights into account when shaping horizontal relations is justified in a number of ways.[3] First, it is said that, at present, private entities breach the constitutional rights of an individual more often than they are breached by states, particularly those with a democratic system. The assumption that private entities are not bound by constitutional rights would mean that the need to protect these rights in democratic states – given that such rights are respected by public authorities as a matter of policy – might prove superfluous. Secondly, it is pointed out that, because dignity is the source of constitutional rights, the latter – like dignity – must be protected in a universal and uniform, rather than partial and selective, manner. Thus, the application of constitutional rights cannot be restrained only to

---

[1] The process of impacting the private law by constitutional norms is known as the 'constitutionalization of the private law.' Cf. M. Safjan, "Efekt horyzontalny praw podstawowych w prawie prywatnym: autonomia woli a zasada równego traktowania," *Kwartalnik Prawa Prywatnego*, 2 (2009), p. 300; O.O. Cherednychenko, "Fundamental rights and private law: A relationship of subordination or complementarity?," *Ultrecht Law Review*, 3 (2007), p. 4; H. Nieuwenhuis, "Fundamental rights talk. An enrichment of legal discourse in private law?" (in:) T. Barkhuysen, P.D. Lindenbergh (eds.), *Constitutionalisation of Private Law*, Leiden 2006, p. 9; J. Smits, "Private law and fundamental rights: A sceptical view" (in:) T. Barkhuysen, P.D. Lindenbergh (eds.), *Constitutionalisation of Private Law*, Leiden 2006, p. 9–22.

[2] As highlighted by O.O. Cherednychenko, as a result of the process of the constitutionalization of the private law, fundamental rights can no longer remain in isolation from the private law. Cf. O.O. Cherednychenko, "Fundamental rights and private law...," p. 1.

[3] For their synthetic comparison, cf. A. Barak, "Constitutional human rights and private law," *Review of Constitutional Studies*, 2 (1996), p. 228 et. seq.

the sphere of relations between an individual and the state, while considering that the same rights might be violated in relations between individuals. Thirdly, constitutional rights are at present an indispensable element of a democratic constitution, and the latter is no longer merely a normative act that governs the organization of the state and the principles of functioning of public authorities. The constitution enters into new areas of social life, interfering with the shape of relations between employers and employees, parents and children, and consumers and entrepreneurs. Accordingly, given that the extent of constitutional regulation is expanding, the scope of constitutional rights should not be limited solely to relations between an individual and the state. Fourthly, the need to incorporate constitutional rights into horizontal relations is justified by the necessity for the state to offer an elementary sense of justice and protection to individuals. A condition under which a constitutional right can be violated with impunity by a private entity undermines the importance of this right and violates the most intuitive belief about the need for its protection.

On the other hand, the horizontal effect of constitutional rights has always posed a challenge for the private law, and this has not changed. This is because, since this concept restrains the widely understood sphere of an individual's freedom and requires the latter to take into account the constitutional rights of other entities while taking action. This, on the other hand, raises the question of whether the horizontal effect of constitutional rights can be reconciled with the basic principles of private law, such as the principle of the autonomy of the will or the principle of the freedom of contract.[4] As Marek Safjan has noted, 'the debate centered around the question of the necessary minimum degree of *equilibrium* in private-legal relations, all while respecting the principles of autonomy and freedom, is one of the most vital questions put forward today within the frame of theoretical reflections, but also in the case law, as to the fundamental aspect of applying constitutional rules in private law.'[5]

Thus, despite the prevailing consensus that constitutional rights should have an impact upon horizontal relations, two major issues associated with this position remain disputed. First, it remains to be clarified how the horizontal effect of constitutional rights should be ensured. Secondly, there is the question of the extent to which they should be taken into account in rela-

---

[4] L. Fastrich, "Human rights and private law" (in:) K.P. Ziegler (ed.), *Human Rights and Private Law. Privacy as Autonomy*, Oregon 2007, p. 29; A. Guckelberger, "Die Drittwirkung der Grundrechte Juristische Schulung," 12 (2013), p. 1153; T. Langer, *Die Problematik der Geltung der Grundrechte zwischen Privaten*, Frankfurt 1998, p. 62–64.

[5] M. Safjan, "Efekt horyzontalny praw podstawowych...," p. 297.

tions between private entities. As regards the first contentious issue, which Robert Alexy described as 'the problem of construction,'[6] it should be noted that different countries have adopted differing models regarding the horizontal effect of constitutional rights. The models most frequently mentioned in the legal literature on the subject include models of the direct horizontal application and the indirect horizontal application of constitutional rights and the protective responsibilities of the state in horizontal relations. As regards the second contentious issue, described by R. Alexy as the 'problem of collision,'[7] it should be noted that conflicts between the constitutional rights of parties who are in horizontal relations are currently resolved in a similar way within different jurisdictions. The inability of each of the parties to exercise conflicting constitutional rights to the full extent of their binding force and application creates a need to balance them in a way that will allow them to be exercised to the greatest extent possible. The mechanism for balancing the values that underpin constitutional rights does, in fact, reveal certain differences within the individual models for the horizontal application of constitutional rights, which will also be described and clarified in this book.

Despite volumes of research on the subject, the problem of the horizontal effect of individuals' rights continues to enjoy steadfast interest in Western literature, as evidenced by the recent collective studies that analyze this issue from a comparative perspective.[8] These collective works have failed, however, to present the approach of Polish jurisprudence and judicature. It is a fact that, in Poland, the problem of the horizontal application of constitutional rights has so far been only sporadically taken up in the legal literature. It has not been considered to a wider extent in the case law or directly made the subject of constitutional regulation. The Constitution of the Republic of Poland is nonetheless applied in the courts' jurisprudence and influences the shape of horizontal relations. Polish courts also apply solutions specific to the particular models for the horizontal application of constitutional rights, although they do not explicitly refer to those models.

These circumstances inspired me to initiate research on the problem of the horizontal effect of individual rights, the results of which I presented in

---

[6] R. Alexy, *Theorie der Grundrechte*, Baden-Baden 1985, p. 480.

[7] Ibidem.

[8] A. Sajo, R. Uitz (eds.), *The Constitution in Private Relation: Expanding Constitutionalism*, Utrecht 2005; T. Barkhuysen, S.D. Lindenbergh (eds.), *Constitutionalisation of Private Law*, Leiden 2006; D. Oliver, J. Fedtke (eds.), *Human Rights and the Private Sphere. A Comparative Study*, New York 2007; M. Faure, A. van der Walt (eds.), *Globalization and Private Law. The Way Forward*, Cheltenham 2010; E. Reid, D. Visser (eds.), *Private Law and Human Rights. Bringing Rights Home in Scotland and South Africa*, Edinburgh 2013.

a monograph that was published in 2014 by Jagiellonian University Press [Wydawnictwo Uniwersytetu Jagiellońskiego].[9] I carried out this research within the frame of a grant from the Foundation for Polish Science [Fundacja na rzecz Nauki Polskiej] for a research project under the title 'The horizontal dimension of the constitutional rights in a comparative perspective.' This book is an abbreviated version of that monograph, and its purpose is to make the results of my research known to English-speaking readers and to disseminate the approach of the Polish judicature and jurisprudence on the horizontal effect of individual rights beyond the boundaries of Poland. I would like to take this opportunity to thank my reviewer Professor Piotr Tuleja for his valuable remarks, which contributed to the final formulation of this monograph.

This monograph comprises five chapters, in which I have analyzed the problem of the horizontal effect of individual rights within the Polish constitutional reality.

In the first chapter, I ponder the question of why the problem of the horizontal effect of individual rights was, in fact, not contemplated at all in Poland's jurisprudence until the 1980s, and why it is not expressly laid down in the Polish Constitution, despite a relevant clause being proposed during legislative work on the draft constitution. A determination of the reasons why these proposals were eventually rejected by the Constitutional Commission of the National Assembly allowed me to reconstruct the actual intentions of the constitutional legislator. It turned out that the decision to abandon the said clause was not a purposeful action of the legislator, and therefore, nothing stands in the way of assuming that the horizontal application of constitutional rights fits within the framework of the Polish Constitution.

In the second chapter, I analyze the way individuals' rights and freedoms are regulated in the Constitution of the Republic of Poland. The purpose of this analysis is to determine whether the Polish Constitution covers rights or freedoms that may have a horizontal dimension, as well as the entities that are the holders of such rights and those that are beholden. However, the invocation of constitutional rights by the holders of those rights in disputes with other private entities first requires a finding that constitutional provisions can be directly applied. Accordingly, the focus of my further consideration, contained in chapter three, is the principle of direct application of the Polish Constitution, which is provided for in Article 8 para. 2 thereof. I have considered it of crucial importance to determine what constitutes the direct application of the Constitution of the Republic of Poland and what practical

---

[9] M. Florczak-Wątor, *Horyzontalny wymiar praw konstytucyjnych*, Kraków 2014.

form it may take when examining the horizontal dimension of constitutional rights.[10] The concept of the direct application of the Constitution, in such a broad sense, which has been adopted by the Polish legal jurisprudence and judicature, constitutes the 'axis' upon which different models of the horizontal application of constitutional rights can be built.

In the fourth chapter, I deliberate upon the problem of the scope of the horizontal application of constitutional rights and the related issue of the collision of constitutional rights. It is a specific feature of horizontal relations that both of the parties are beneficiaries of constitutional rights and freedoms, and both rely on those rights and freedoms, demanding their protection. Last, but not least, in chapter five, I distinguish three basic models for the horizontal operation of individual rights in an attempt to determine their applicability within the Polish constitutional reality. The scope of my research covered the model for the direct horizontal application of individual's rights, the model for the indirect horizontal application of these rights and the model for the protective responsibilities of the state. In different countries these models are often applied in a parallel and complementary manner. They are not competitive towards one another; there is no need to select one optimum model that would preclude the application of other models. In my deliberations I have omitted the state action model recognizing that given the form in which it is employed in the United States, it has little applicability under the Polish Constitution.

---

[10] Likewise, *cf.* A. Drozd, "Drittwirkung der Grundrechte im polnischen Recht mit besonderer Berücksichtigung des Arbeitsrechts", *Deutsche-Polnische Juristen-Zeitschrift*, 2008, p. 28; B. Skwara, "Horyzontalne obowiązywanie praw człowieka. Rozważania teoretyczno-prawne" (in:) J. Jaskiernia (ed.), *Efektywność europejskiego systemu ochrony praw człowieka. Ewolucja i uwarunkowania systemu ochrony praw człowieka*, Toruń 2012, p. 385; S. Jarosz-Żukowska, "Problem horyzontalnego stosowania norm konstytucyjnych dotyczących wolności i praw jednostki w świetle Konstytucji RP" (in:) M. Jabłoński (ed.), *Wolności i prawa jednostki w Konstytucji RP*, Warszawa 2010, p. 189.

Chapter 1

THE PROBLEM OF THE HORIZONTAL EFFECT
OF CONSTITUTIONAL RIGHTS DURING THE DRAFTING
OF THE POLISH CONSTITUTION

1.1. The Period Preceding the Drafting of the Constitution

Although after World War II, the issue of the horizontal effect of constitutional rights was widely discussed across many European countries, particularly in Germany and Switzerland, it was basically not taken up at all in the Polish legal literature. The reason for the lack of interest in this subject in Poland was above all the politicization of the then binding Constitution of 1952 as well as disrespect for the rights of the individual that was laid down in that Constitution and the marginalization of those rights by communist authorities. That Constitution was denied a normative quality through the recognition that it was not apt for direct application. Its norms were believed to be too general, and to always require concretization by statutes. The Constitution itself did not confer any specific protective tools to individuals in the event of the violation of the rights or freedoms enshrined in it. The approach of the jurisprudence during that period was shaped by a resolution of the Supreme Court of 12 February 1955, Ref. No. I CO 4/55, which stated: 'Constitutional norms construe basic legal principles, constituting the axis of the suprastructure of laws, which as a rule is unsuitable for direct practical application in everyday life of the society, unless expounded in statutes and other normative acts.' Accordingly, since the applicability of the Constitution was challenged even in vertical relations (between the individual and the state), it was completely pointless to consider its application in horizontal relations (between individuals).

The absence of discussion regarding the horizontal effect of constitutional rights was also a consequence of the perception of the Constitution of 1952 by the then contemporary jurisprudence as a normative act belonging to 'state law' and regulating relations between the individual and the state. It should be noted that, in post-war socialist Poland, the distinction between the sphere of public law and private law was not as clearly drawn as in other countries in Europe at that time. Moreover, the public law dominated and marginalized the private law. There were various reasons for this. First, Polish law, during that period, remained under the strong influence of Soviet law, which rejected the division into public and private law, recognizing that such a division finds its justification only in relation to the law of the so-called pre-socialist formations. Secondly, denying the need for private ownership and emphasizing the importance of collective ownership also brought about the expansion of public law into spheres that were regarded as falling under private law in Western European countries. As the Polish legal scholar Andrzej Stelmachowski wrote: 'Lenin's famous statement that "We do not recognize anything «private», and regard everything in the economic sphere as falling under public and not private law" laconically expressed the very essence of socialist type of law (...) The doctrinal division into public law and private law lost its *raison d'être* in socialist state.' Thirdly, during the era of the Polish Peoples' Republic (PRL), the private interests of individuals were subordinate to, and even identified with, the interests of the entire society. This ruled out a division of law into public and private based on the criterion of interest recognized by Ulpian, according to which the law that protects the interests of the state is the public law and the law that protects the interests of individuals is the private law. In a socialist state, the indistinguishability between private and public law based on this criterion was a consequence that was typical for socialism, i.e. the harmonious compatibility between social and personal interests. As a result, the perception of certain behaviors as private, autonomous, and free from state regulation was not as strongly rooted in Polish society as it was in the West.

The need for a new perspective on the problem of the relations between private entities was, so to speak, triggered in Poland by the socio-economic changes accompanying the political transformation that took place in the 1990s. On the one hand, the state began to transfer tasks that it had previously implemented on an exclusive basis to private entities in fields such as education, health care, public transportation and building public utility facilities. Thus, private entities began to implement tasks of a public nature, which was a completely new phenomenon, given the earlier omnipotence of the state that was quite typical of the socialist system. On the other hand, at that time, stronger and stronger private entities that were endowed with a state-like capacity to subjugate individuals began to spring up and operate in Poland, namely all kinds of international corporations, supranational non-governmental organizations and global regulators. Their classification as private entities became increasingly debatable over time due to their growing ability to act in a wide public sphere. In the era of privatization, when private entities often fulfill public functions, availing themselves of the state powers that authorize their actions, it is not easy to determine exactly where the public sphere ends and the private sphere begins. Even institutions that are traditionally perceived as being the backbone of the private sphere, such as private ownership, may take on a public nature. The more a private owner transfers, for profit, his own property for public use, the more he must surrender to the limitations of his own rights due to the need to protect the rights of the people who use his property. This is an example of circumstances in which the public and the private sector overlap, because private property that is made available to the public loses its exclusively private nature. This process of blurring the boundaries between public and private law, i.e. the mutual interaction between the two spheres of law and their intermingling, began to be called the 'publicization of private law' in Polish legal literature.

As a result of all of the phenomena described above, the first studies on the problem of the horizontal effect of constitutional rights, which reported the approaches adopted in foreign legal literature and jurisprudence did not appear in Polish legal writings until the 1980s. It was under the influence of these publications that this issue became the subject of debate during the drafting of the Constitution that is currently in force, which was enacted in 1997.

1.2. Solutions Adopted in Drafts of the Constitution

Not all of the draft versions of the Constitution incorporated the aspect of the horizontal effect of constitutional rights; nonetheless, it was present in most of them. The first draft, in which the clause on the horizontal effectiveness of constitutional rights appeared, was the text drafted in 1990 by a team of experts headed by S. Zawadzki.[11] According to the wording of Article 36 thereof, 'Freedoms and rights enshrined in the Constitution shall apply appropriately to relations between natural and legal persons, accordingly to their nature.' A year later, the Constitutional Commission of the Sejm [the lower house of the Polish Parliament] of the tenth term adopted a draft version that contained a similar solution. Article 17 of that version read: 'Rights and freedoms enshrined in the Constitution shall apply to relations between private

---

[11] The draft was published in a separate publication by Warsaw University and in the Bulletin of the Constitutional Commission of the National Assembly (Biuletyn Komisji Konstytucyjnej Zgromadzenia Narodowego). *Cf.* Konstytucja Rzeczypospolitej Polskiej. Projekt, Warsaw, October 1990 and Bulletin of the Constitutional Committee no. XII of 1990, p. 9–23.

entities, accordingly to their nature.'[12] The first of those drafts never became the subject of a legislative initiative, and parliamentary work on the second draft was discontinued after it was agreed that the new Constitution would be passed by the first parliament to be elected in a fully democratic way.

After the elections of 1993, work on the Constitution was resumed. Out of the seven draft versions of the Constitution then submitted, one draft version explicitly envisaged the horizontal effect of constitutional rights, the second openly precluded such horizontal effect, while yet another contained a legal regulation that could have been interpreted in various ways with respect to this issue. The remaining draft versions did not address the issue at all.

The draft Constitution that expressly endowed constitutional rights with a horizontal dimension was a draft by a group of Members of Parliament and Senators, including members of the parliamentary club of the Polish People's Party [Polskie Stronnictwo Ludowe], the MPs' group of the Labor Union [Unia Pracy], the German Minority [Mniejszość Niemiecka], the Party of Pensioners and Retirees "The Hope" [Partia Rencistów i Emerytów "Nadzieja"] and non-attached MPs.[13] Article 17 of this draft read as follows: 'Rights and freedoms enshrined in the Constitution shall apply to relations between private entities, accordingly to their nature.' It was thus a proposal that was identical to that brought forward in the tenth term of the Sejm by the then acting Constitutional Commission.

The draft Constitution containing an approach to the horizontal effect of constitutional rights that was not entirely clear was the one prepared by the Constitutional Commission of the first term of the Senate. Article 16 of this draft contained the following wording: 'The Republic of Poland shall ensure judicial legal protection to any person whose rights and freedoms enshrined in the Constitution have been violated, also when such a violation was committed by persons acting in an official capacity.'[14] The final part of this clause can be understood in two ways. First, it may be deemed that constitutional rights and freedoms can be violated also by persons not acting in an official capacity (and therefore by private entities), which would mean that this draft accepted the principle of horizontal effect of constitutional rights. Secondly, the cited fragment of Article 16 could be interpreted as meaning that constitutional rights and freedoms can be violated by public authorities as well as 'by persons acting in an official capacity.' Given such an interpretation, it should be concluded that this clause precluded the horizontal effect of consti-

---

[12] *Projekty konstytucyjne 1989–1991*, edited for print by M. Kallas, Warsaw 1992, p. 22.
[13] *Projekty konstytucji 1993–1997*, edited for print by R. Chruściak, Warsaw 1997, p. 190.
[14] Ibidem, p. 142.

tutional rights. In both cases, the word 'also' placed before the phrase 'persons acting in an official capacity' suggested that there was a certain obvious group of violators of constitutional rights and freedoms, which there was no need to mention. It remains an open question, however, whether, in light of the said Article 16, this obvious group of violators was intended to cover state authorities or individuals.

The draft Constitution submitted in 1994 by Lech Wałęsa, who was then President of the Republic of Poland, containing the Charter of Rights and Freedoms as its integral part, directly excluded the horizontal effect of constitutional rights. Its application was limited to vertical relations only. Art. 1 para. 1 of the Charter pronounced: 'This Charter defines relations between persons who fall under the law of the Republic of Poland and public authorities.' The statement of reasons for this draft read: 'The Charter regulates the relations between an individual and the state rather than relations between people or between state authorities. It is a collection of rights, the respect for which a citizen may enforce from the state through a court of law.'[15]

1.3. Discussion on the Inclusion of the Horizontal Effect Clause

Eventually, the fate of the clause on the horizontal effect of constitutional rights was determined at the meeting of the Citizens' Rights and Duties Subcommission of the Constitutional Commission of the National Assembly held on November 30, 1994. On that day, two versions of a provision that contained such a clause were considered. The first version was: 'Freedoms and rights enshrined in the Constitution shall apply to relations between private entities, accordingly to their nature.' The second version read as follows: 'Freedoms and rights enshrined in the Constitution shall apply appropriately to relations between citizens and legal persons, accordingly to their nature.' Thus, the differences between these two variants of the provision were editorial, rather than substantive, in nature. The mere fact, however, that two potential variants of this provision were considered leads to the conclusion that its inclusion into the text of the new Constitution seemed preordained, and only its wording was contested.

During the meeting of the said Subcommission, however, a discussion evolved that ultimately induced the Subcommission members to remove the clause on the horizontal effect of individual's rights from the draft Constitu-

---

[15] Ibidem, p. 89.

tion. When proceeding to examine this item of the parliamentary agenda, the chairman of the Subcommission, MP J. Gwiżdż, announced that in his opinion 'it is a redundant provision.'[16] In turn, the President's representative, A. Rzepliński, added: 'This provision reflects a certain view prevailing amongst researchers. Yet it does not enjoy a great support in the human rights doctrine.' Considering that 'this provision "distorts" the responsibility of public authorities related to civil rights and freedoms,' A. Rzepliński proposed that it not be included. Because none of the MPs or Senators were against striking-off that provision, it was removed from the draft Constitution during that particular meeting of the Subcommission.[17]

In the end, the uniform text of the Constitution of the Republic of Poland, which the Constitutional Commission completed on June 19, 1996, did not contain a provision on the horizontal or vertical effect of constitutional rights. The removal of the said clause from the draft of the Constitution of the Republic of Poland was viewed in a different way in the legal literature; diametrically different conclusions have also been drawn from this fact.[18]

1.4. Conclusions Impacting the Interpretation of Constitutional Provisions

It does not follow from the course of the discussion during the meeting of the Subcommission of the Constitutional Commission of the National Assembly, during which the proposed clause on the horizontal effect of constitutional rights was removed from the Constitution, that the reason for this decision was a belief of the parliamentarians or experts of the Constitutional Commission of the National Assembly that constitutional rights apply only to vertical relations. The opinion regarding the redundancy of this clause that was expressed by the Chairman of the Subcommission can be interpreted in various ways. Redundancy may, in fact, mean that either there is no need to 'write down' in the Polish Constitution something as obvious, or that there is no need to include something in it that does not exist or does not matter in

---

[16] Bulletin of the Constitutional Commission of the National Assembly (Biuletyn Komisji Konstytucyjnej Zgromadzenia Narodowego), X (1995), p. 130.

[17] Ibidem.

[18] Cf. L. Wiśniewski, "Tor przeszkód projektu nowej konstytucji," *Rzeczpospolita*, June 20, 1996; L. Wiśniewski, "Dla kogo konstytucja," *Rzeczpospolita*, October 9, 1996; W. Sadurski, "Konstytucja Muminków," *Rzeczpospolita*, June 10, 1996.

practice. Also, the view of A. Rzepliński regarding the risk of 'distorting' the responsibility of public authorities for violations of constitutional rights and freedoms did not deny their horizontal effect. Hence, the non-inclusion of that clause in the Constitution of the Republic of Poland does not rule out the adoption of the thesis that constitutional rights have a horizontal dimension. As has already been emphasized by M. Piechowiak, after the Constitution entered into force, the rights of the people are 'by their nature open to different entities, depending on the nature of the given right and the circumstances, while the constitution, also by its nature, does not govern only an individual's relation with a state, but provides the grounds to organize the entire social life. With a right formulation of fundamental rights and freedoms, there is therefore no need for introducing (...) a formula' directly relating to the horizontal application of human rights.[19]

---

[19] M. Piechowiak, "Pojęcie praw człowieka" (in:) L. Wiśniewski (ed.), *Podstawowe prawa jednostki i ich sądowa ochrona*, Warszawa 1997, p. 31.

Chapter 2

HOLDERS OF CONSTITUTIONAL RIGHTS
AND FREEDOMS

2.1. Regulation of Rights and Freedoms in the Polish Constitution

The Constitution of the Republic of Poland enshrines a sizeable list of the rights and freedoms of an individual, which is itemized in Chapter II, immediately following the general principles. The emphasis on these questions in the Constitution's systematics proves the great importance attached to them by the constitutional legislator. Chapter II of the Constitution starts with the three guiding principles, i.e. the principles of dignity, equality and freedom. An inherent and inalienable human dignity is identified as the source of the individual's rights and freedoms. It does not, however, make these freedoms absolute, because almost all constitutional rights and freedoms may be restricted by the public authorities, subject to the conditions identified in Art. 31 para. 3 of the Constitution. The restrictions can be introduced only in statutes and only to the extent to which they are necessary in a democratic state for the protection of security and the public order, the natural environment, health, public morals, and the rights and freedoms of other persons. However, these restrictions cannot violate the essence of such rights and freedoms.

The rights and freedoms of an individual are worded in the Constitution in various ways. Some provisions state that a given person 'shall have the right,' and in others legal protection is accorded to specific interests of an individual, such as his work or property. Other provisions protect a certain freedom without naming the person who enjoys it, using the following expressions 'freedom (...) shall be ensured' (e.g. Art. 49, Art. 50, Art. 61 para. 1, Art. 62 para. 1) or 'the Republic of Poland shall ensure protection' (Art. 38, Art. 72 para. 1). Yet another group of constitutional provisions place emphasis on the universality of certain freedoms, with the expression 'freedom shall be ensured to everyone' (e.g. Art. 52 para. 1, Art. 53 para. 1, Art. 54 para. 1, Art. 57). However, none of these kinds of provisions have given rise to any major problems in decoding constitutional rights and freedoms.

But such problems have arisen with respect to some of the provisions in the subchapter on 'Economic, Social and Cultural Freedoms and Rights,' which generally do not expressly mention any rights or freedoms of the individual, but rather, address the state's obligations. These provisions contain the so-called program norms (also referred to as principles of the state's policy), which are addressed to public authorities and direct them to take measures intended to achieve specified socio-economic goals.[20] What indirectly follows from these norms is a ban on taking measures that prevent the achievement of those goals. Some program norms merely set the desirable socio-economic goals, but others also identify the means that must be used to achieve them. An example of the latter kind can be found in Art. 65 para. 5 of the Polish Constitution, according to which the 'Public authorities shall pursue policies aiming at full, productive employment by implementing programs to combat unemployment, including the organization of and support for occupational advice and training, as well as public works and economic intervention.' Polish legal scholars disagree on whether program norms are a source of constitutional rights and freedoms that can be enforced by individuals. On the one hand, no subjective rights are expressly formulated in these provisions and sometimes it is even difficult to establish what specifically an individual could demand from the public authorities on the basis of such a provision. This would lead to the conclusion that program norms are not a source of subjective rights. On the other hand, the provisions in question are to be found in Chapter II, entitled 'The Freedoms, Rights and Obligations of Persons and Citizens,' while Art. 81 of the Polish Constitution expressly states that the 'rights' specified in those very provisions 'may be asserted subject to limitations specified by statute.' These are at least two important arguments to support the thesis that program norms can be the source of subjective rights.

The case law of the Constitutional Tribunal also does not provide an unequivocal answer to the question of whether a specific subjective right can be derived from a program norm. It follows from some Constitutional Tribunal judgments that a program norm gives no grounds for decoding specific le-

---

[20] On the subject of program norms, *cf.* T. Gizbert-Studnicki, A. Grabowski, "Normy programowe w konstytucji" (in:) *Charakter i struktura norm Konstytucji*, Warszawa 1997; P. Sarnecki, "Normy programowe w Konstytucji i odpowiadające im wolności obywatelskie" (in:) L. Garlicki, A. Szmyt (eds.), *Sześć lat Konstytucji Rzeczypospolitej Polskiej. Doświadczenia i inspiracje*, Warszawa 2003, p. 252–262; M. Florczak-Wątor, "Możliwość kontrolowania przez TK swobody ustawodawcy w zakresie realizacji norm programowych," *Przegląd Sejmowy*, 4 (2009), p. 111–12

gal rights of an individual,[21] while according to other Constitutional Tribunal judgments, in certain situations, program norms contained in the Constitution can also give rise to rights and freedoms of individuals.[22] In addition, in some Constitutional Tribunal case law, one can find a view according to which program norms are the 'germ' of rights and freedoms, setting their minimum content and the corresponding minimum obligations of the state.[23] I believe that we cannot completely rule out the possibility of inferring subjective rights from provisions containing program norms. If only the content of such provisions enables the reconstruction of all of the elements of the subjective right, their program character should not be an obstacle.

Constitutional rights and freedoms can stem not only from the provisions included in Chapter II of the Polish Constitution, but also from provisions in other parts of the Constitution. An example is the freedom of economic activity, regulated in Art. 20 and Art. 22 of the Polish Constitution, in Chapter I entitled 'The Republic,' and the right to stand as a candidate in parliamentary elections (Art. 99 of the Polish Constitution) and in presidential elections (Art. 127 para. 3), regulated in the chapters concerning the organization and functioning of such authorities. Moreover, the Tribunal assumes that even provisions that do not directly express a certain right or freedom can be their source. An example is Art. 2 of the Polish Constitution, pursuant to which the Republic of Poland is a democratic state ruled by law and implementing the principles of social justice. The Constitutional Tribunal assumes that this provision could be an independent basis of review in proceedings triggered by a constitutional complaint, if from this provision, the applicant derives rights or freedoms that are not enshrined in other constitutional provisions.[24] A basis of review in proceedings concerning constitutional complaints can only be a constitutional provision that establishes specific rights or freedoms.

---

[21] Decisions of the Constitutional Tribunal: of January 20, 2009, Ref. No. Ts 240/07. Of February 6, 2002, Ref. No. Ts 104/01; of September 21, 1999, Ref. No. Ts 57/99; of June 26, 2002, Ref. No. SK 1/02; of December 22, 2008, Ref. No. Ts 216/08; of June 29, 2011, Ref. No. Ts 214/10; of January 17, 2012, Ref. No. Ts 294/11; of October 24, 2006, Ref. No. Ts 158/06; of January 5, 2010, Ref. No. Ts 63/09; of April 29, 2008, Ref. No. Ts 203/07.

[22] Judgments of the Constitutional Tribunal: of May 11, 2011, Ref. No. SK 11/09; of November 13, 2007, Ref. No. P 42/06; decision of July 15, 2009, Ref. No. Ts 214/07.

[23] *Cf.* e.g. judgment of the Constitutional Tribunal of March 11, 2008, Ref. No. SK 58/06 and decision of September 10, 2009, Ref. No. Ts 342/08.

[24] *Cf.* e.g. decisions of the Constitutional Tribunal: of January 24, 2001, Ref. No. Ts 129/00; of March 6, 2001, Ref. No. Ts 199/00; of June 21, 2001, Ref. No. Ts 187/00; of August 10, 2001, Ref. No. Ts 56/01; of June 26, 2002, Ref. No. SK 1/02 and judgments of the Constitutional Tribunal: of December 12, 2001, Ref. No. SK 26/01; of July 10, 2007, Ref. No. SK 50/06; of October 28, 2010, Ref. No. SK 19/09.

2.2. The Principle of Universal Enjoyment of Constitutional Rights and Freedoms

Pursuant to Art. 37 of the Constitution, 'Anyone, being under the authority of the Polish State, shall enjoy the freedoms and rights ensured by the Constitution;' however exceptions to this principle with respect to foreigners may be specified by statute. The aforementioned provision articulates the principle of the universal enjoyment of constitutional rights and freedoms. As for its scope, this principle applies to 'freedoms and rights ensured by the Constitution,' and thus, not solely to those regulated in Chapter II, which includes the aforementioned Art. 37. In terms of its beneficiaries, the principle of the universal enjoyment of constitutional rights and freedoms covers anyone who is 'under the authority of the Republic of Poland,' but foreigners may be subjected to limitations in its application. Thus, the universal enjoyment of constitutional rights and freedoms is subject to two reservations. The first is the requirement that one must be under the authority of the Polish state, and the other concerns foreigners.

Most constitutional rights and freedoms, in accordance with the aforementioned principle of universality, have a general character, which means that anyone within the sphere of influence of Polish law may enjoy them. Thus, first of all, any human being is a holder of constitutional rights and freedoms, which follows both from the title of Chapter II and its individual provisions. The constitutional legislator uses several notions to define that holder: 'person' ('human being'), 'anyone,' 'no one,' 'everyone' and 'all persons.' The first notion is used in provisions that concern the dignity of the person (Art. 30 and Preamble), the freedom of the person (Art. 31) and the legal protection of the life of a human being (Art. 38). In other constitutional provisions, the remaining phrases are used to express the universality of rights and freedoms. They seem to be more capacious terms than 'person/ human being,' because they can refer not only to natural persons, but also legal persons and other organizational units. Nonetheless, this does not mean that all of the constitutional rights and freedoms that are enjoyed by 'anyone,' 'no one' or 'everyone' concern the same groups of addressees. The group of persons to which they apply is additionally determined by the character of the given right or freedom. Some constitutional rights and freedoms by definition apply to natural persons only, and thus, terms such as 'anyone,' 'no one' or 'everyone' will be used according to a narrow meaning to define this group of entities. On the other hand, some constitutional rights and freedoms may also be enjoyed by legal persons or other organizational units. In this case, the aforementioned terms 'anyone,' 'no one' or 'everyone' will be used in a broad sense, covering all entities capable of enjoying a given right or freedom in their interest.[25] First, these will be include legal persons, which, in light of the civil law, have legal capacity, that is, they can have rights and obligations. As the Constitutional Tribunal stated in its judgment of May 7, 2001, Ref. No. K 19/00, 'A legal person may be the holder of constitutional public subjective rights, because this enables a fuller implementation of these rights by individual natural persons. This is the *ratio legis* of including legal persons in the group of persons enjoying e.g. freedom of association, freedom of economic activity or right to protection of ownership.'

Legal personality in the civil-law sense is not, however, a condition for having freedoms and rights in the sphere of constitutional law.[26] Therefore, these rights and freedoms may also be enjoyed by organizational units that are not legal persons, or even by groups of natural persons that are not organized in a way that allows their recognition as units of this kind. I will return to the problem of the latter entities further in this book.

2.3. Citizen as a Holder of Constitutional Rights and Freedoms

The aforementioned principle of universality expressed in Art. 37 para. 1 of the Constitution does not apply when the constitutional provision narrows down the group of entities enjoying a given right or freedom. This concerns, in the first place, the rights and freedoms that the Constitution confers on citizens. In this context, we should observe that citizens, in addition to persons, are the second group of entities mentioned in the title of Chapter II of the Constitution, which reads: 'The Freedoms, Rights and Obligations of Persons and Citizens.' This title does not refer to separate terms identifying two completely different groups of holders of constitutional rights and freedoms.

---

[25] This distinction is accepted by legal scholars. *Cf.* J. Trzciński, "Zakres podmiotowy i podstawa skargi konstytucyjnej" (in:) J. Trzciński (ed.), *Skarga konstytucyjna*, Warszawa 2000, p. 49–51; B. Szmulik, *Skarga konstytucyjna na tle porównawczym*, Warszawa 2006, p. 113–117; L. Jamróz, *Skarga konstytucyjna. Wstępne rozpoznanie*, Białystok 2011, p. 71. It also appears in the Constitutional Tribunal case law. *Cf.* e.g. the judgment of June 8, 1999, Ref. No. SK 12/98, in which the Tribunal held: 'It seems (…) obvious that certain rights, such as the right of ownership, or freedoms, such as freedom to engage in business activity – by the nature of the economic system – apply not only to natural persons, but also to economic entities.'

[26] Decisions of the Constitutional Tribunal: of February 23, 2005, Ref. No. Ts 35/04; of April 6, 2005, Ref. No. Ts 9/05.

The terms 'persons' and 'citizens' denote a broader or narrower group of entities enjoying constitutional rights or duties. The meanings of these terms overlap only partially, because a citizen is always a person, while not every person is a citizen, because he may be a stateless person having no citizenship.

In addition to the term 'citizen,' some constitutional provisions also refer to 'Polish citizen.' In pondering the relationship between these terms, one should reach the conclusion that 'citizen' is not a broader term that also covers citizens of other states, along with Polish citizens. Each time the notion of 'citizen' is used, the constitutional legislator means Polish citizens. So, regardless of whether the holder of the constitutional right was referred to as a citizen or a Polish citizen, exactly the same group of persons is meant. Yet legal scholars have pointed out that the rights and freedoms reserved in the Polish Constitution for 'Polish citizens' are closely tied with the essence of citizenship understood as a special legal bond between an individual and the state. The rights and freedoms granted to 'citizens,' without the stipulation that they concern Polish citizens, do not display such a close bond with the state. On this premise, one could formulate a thesis that these two groups constituting rights and freedoms differ in terms of permitting the group of their holders to be extended in sub-constitutional acts. Rights reserved in the Constitution for Polish citizens – unlike those reserved for citizens – cannot be granted in statutory law to foreigners and stateless persons.[27] As regards rights reserved for citizens, such extra-constitutional extensions of the groups constituting the holders of a right or freedom produces the result that a given right (freedom) is a constitutional right (freedom) for Polish citizens and statutory right (freedom) for foreigners and stateless persons. This in turn means that when granting a given right to foreigners, the legislator can freely shape its substance and limit the said right without taking into account the conditions listed in Art. 31 para. 3 of the Constitution, and foreigners cannot claim the protection of these rights by means of a constitutional complaint. This seems to be the only rational reason for the fact that the constitutional legislator uses the notions of both 'citizen' and 'Polish citizen.'

---

[27] Likewise *cf.* M. Jabłoński, "Zakres podmiotowy realizacji praw obywatelskich w Konstytucji RP z 2.4.1997 r." (in:) B. Banaszak, A. Preisner (eds.), *Prawa i wolności obywatelskie w Konstytucji RP*, Warszawa 2002, p. 150–151. Differently K. Wojtyczek, "Konstytucyjne regulacje systemu wyborczego w III Rzeczypospolitej" (in:) F. Rymarz (ed.), *10 lat demokratycznego prawa wyborczego Rzeczypospolitej Polskiej (1990-2000)*, Warszawa 2000, p. 130.

2.4. Special Definitions of Holders of Constitutional Rights and Freedoms

Holding Polish citizenship is not the only factor narrowing down the scope of rights and freedoms enshrined in the constitutional provisions, because some rights and freedoms may be enjoyed by natural persons – regardless of whether they are Polish citizens – who have a feature that distinguishes them from other persons. This feature may be permanent or temporary. In the latter case, this constitutionally specified feature may disappear, with the consequence that the holder of a particular constitutional right or freedom subsequently loses that status. Holders of constitutional rights and freedoms distinguished with respect to a certain special feature might include entities described in the constitutional provisions as women and men (Art. 33), parents (Art. 48 para. 1, Art. 70 para. 3), anyone whose Polish origin was confirmed in accordance with statute (Art. 52 para. 5), or foreigners (Art. 56). The rights referred to in these provisions, by their nature, are not universal and apply specifically to persons who belong to clearly defined categories distinguished by a certain common feature.

A separate category of constitutional rights covers those enjoyed by persons in specific situations. Hypothetically, anyone can find themselves in such a situation, regardless of the citizenship he holds. Such rights are held by e.g. anyone deprived of liberty (Art. 41 paras. 2, 4, 5), every detained person (Art. 41 para. 3), or anyone against whom criminal proceedings have been brought (Art. 42 para. 2). It is obvious that the holder of rights of this kind is specified in the universal way as 'everyone/anyone', and the group constituting the holders of the rights is limited by their special situation.

Yet another way to narrow down a group of holders of constitutional rights and freedoms is to relate them to clearly defined entities other than natural persons. The first category of such entities includes communities formed by natural persons, and those communities are not legal persons. In this category we should include national and ethnic minorities, which have the right to establish their own educational and cultural institutions or institutions designed to protect their religious identity and to participate in the resolution of matters connected with their cultural identity (Art. 35 para. 2), and families in difficult material and social circumstances, particularly those with many children or a single parent, which have the right to special assistance from the public authorities (Art. 71 para. 1). The next category of entities that enjoy constitutional rights and freedoms are specific categories of legal persons named by the constitutional legislator. Among such entities we should mention political parties, which enjoy the freedom to function (Art. 11 para. 1), and trade unions, which have the right to organize workers' strikes or other forms of protest (Art. 59 para. 3), as well as institutions which have the right to establish schools and educational development institutions (Art. 70 para. 3). Due to the fact that a legal person is a legal entity that is distinguishable from natural persons, there is no doubt that it is the legal person, not the natural persons who formed it, that benefits from those constitutional rights and freedoms.

2.5. Question of the Constitutional Personality of Entities Performing the Functions of Public Authorities

An entity performing the functions of a public authority cannot be a holder of constitutional rights and freedoms.[28] As the Constitutional Tribunal stated in its judgment of April 8, 2008, Ref. No. SK 80/06, 'The structure of a constitutional right of which a public authority were to be the beneficiary would lead to equating entities that interfere with rights and freedoms with their holders.' A public authority opposing the state would become a party to a competence dispute and not the holder of a given right that is entitled to demand its defense. With respect to state authorities, constitutional provisions determine their powers to act and not their constitutionally safeguarded rights and freedoms.

Thus, state authorities at the central and local levels, as well as units of local self-government (e.g. communes, counties) cannot be holders of constitutional rights and freedoms, because, by their nature, they differ completely from legal persons established by individuals enjoying a constitutionally safeguarded freedom.[29] Local self-government was established in order to discharge public tasks, and to this end was provided with a legal personality and

---

[28] *Cf.* decisions of the Constitutional Tribunal: of October 26, 2001, Ref. No. Ts 72/01; of February 6, 2001, Ref. No. Ts 188/00; of February 6, 2001, Ref. No. Ts 148/00; of December 20, 2007, Ref. No. SK 67/05; of April 6, 2011, Ref. No. SK 21/07. *Cf.* J. Trzciński, "Podmiotowy zakres skargi konstytucyjnej" (in:) L. Garlicki (ed.), *Konstytucja. Wybory. Parlament. Studia ofiarowane Zdzisławowi Jaroszowi*, Warszawa 2000, p. 213; J. Trzciński, "Zakres podmiotowy i podstawa...," p. 53; B. Banaszak, "Skarga konstytucyjna i jej znaczenie w zakresie ochrony praw podstawowych" (in:) L. Wiśniewski (ed.), *Podstawowe prawa jednostki i ich sądowa ochrona*, Warszawa 1997, p. 178.

[29] *Cf.* decisions of the Constitutional Tribunal: of October 12, 2004, Ref. No. Ts 35/04; of October 26, 2001, Ref. No. Ts 72/01; of December 11, 2002, Ref. No. Ts 116/02; of Octo-

independence protected by the courts.[30] Thus, while individuals enjoy their rights as they please, within the limits defined by the law, and these rights are founded on their dignity and freedom, local self-government units enjoy their rights in order to discharge public tasks.[31]

There are doubts as to whether or not political parties should be treated as entities participating in the administration of public authority, which cannot be the beneficiaries of constitutional rights and freedoms. In the judgment issued on November 17, 2010, Ref. No. Ts 256/09, the Constitutional Tribunal ruled that 'Both at the stage of fighting for power and – the more so – at the time of exercising it, parties cannot be perceived as ordinary legal persons, being just voluntary associations of citizens. (…) The activity of political parties undoubtedly takes place on the public plane and their functions are closely related with problems of the law on the system of government (…). Thus, constant correlation with the state translates into political parties obtaining a public-law status.' Consequently, the Constitutional Tribunal held that a political party was not a holder of constitutional rights and freedoms; hence it could not make a constitutional complaint, which is a means of protecting such rights and freedoms. Thus, the Constitutional Tribunal treated political parties as an element of the state's political structure, which it reiterated in its judgment of September 15, 2011, Ref. No. Ts 256/09, stating: 'A political party (…) enjoys its rights in order to influence the state through the discharge of its Constitution-determined tasks in the public sphere. (…) It follows that a political party (…) functioning in the realm of public law (…), does not enjoy the rights or freedoms specified in Chapter II of the Constitution and guaranteed to private entities.' However two months before the issue of this judgment, in the judgment of July 14, 2011, Ref. No. K 9/11, the Constitutional Tribunal took a different stance and recognized that a political party could hold constitutional rights and freedoms. Without distinguishing between entities of public or private law, it stated that 'the freedom of speech, expressed in Art. 54 para. 1 of the Constitution, may be enjoyed by both individuals (natural persons) and collective entities, among them political parties and electoral committees, which after all are made up of natural persons and speak on their behalf.' The above discrepancy leads to the conclusion that,

---

ber 12, 2004, Ref. No. Ts 35/04; of October 3, 2005, Ref. No. Ts 148/05; of December 20, 2007, Ref. No. SK 67/05.

[30] *Cf.* decisions of the Constitutional Tribunal: of October 26, 2001, Ref. No. Ts 72/01; of December 11, 2002, Ref. No. Ts 116/02; of October 12, 2004, Ref. No. Ts 35/04; of October 3, 2005, Ref. No. Ts 148/05; of April 6, 2005, Ref. No. Ts 9/05; of December 20, 2007, Ref. No. SK 67/05.

[31] Decision of the Constitutional Tribunal of February 23, 2005, Ref. No. Ts 35/04.

for the Constitutional Tribunal, whether political parties are entities under constitutional law is a debatable issue.

2.6. Question of Constitutional Personality of Public-Sector Economic Entities

According to the Constitutional Tribunal, public sector economic entities are also among the entities that cannot be beneficiaries of constitutional rights and freedoms. In the judgment dated May 7, 2001, Ref. No. K 19/00, the Tribunal held: 'The freedom formula cannot be used with respect to the state and other public institutions whose direct involvement in, or indirect influence on, the economy cannot be excluded, but whose operations must be governed by a different constitutional regime than the operation of private entities.' On the other hand, in the judgment of April 6, 2011, Ref. No. SK 21/07, examining the constitutional complaint made by electric energy transmission operator Polskie Sieci Elektroenergetyczne SA, the Constitutional Tribunal stated that due to its close link with the state the company could not be regarded as a holder of constitutional rights and freedoms, because 'The operation of public-sector economic entities should serve the state and the discharge of public tasks by it.' In addition, the Constitutional Tribunal pointed out that private entities were free to decide to commence operation, and to choose a kind of business, their legal and organizational form and the manner and scope of doing business, or finally to curtail, suspend or cease their business. Public-sector economic entities do not have such freedom. For a person, the source of rights and freedoms is his dignity. And as the Tribunal stressed in the judgment of May 7, 2001, Ref. No. K 19/00, 'One can hardly maintain that powers granted to various kinds of business operators, which operate based on the substantive-law grounds of public-law entity ownership, and which have been established on the basis of decisions by public authorities (even if such decision have actually been made in forms typical of private law), have a direct link with, or stem from, human dignity.'

The Constitutional Tribunal assumes that the basic element differentiating the position of private entities from that of the state and other public institutions is the substantive-law grounds for their business operations. Thus in its view, an entity pursuing economic activity based entirely on public assets, in particular a sole-shareholder company of the State Treasury, a state-owned enterprise, a unit of local self-government is undoubtedly a public-sector economic entity, which cannot be the holder of constitutional rights and free-doms.[32] However, doubts do appear in determining whether the given right can be held by a mixed-type entity, combining both public and private cap-ital, such as a joint-stock company in which the State Treasury holds shares. This problem was pondered in Constitutional Tribunal case law against the background of cases initiated by the constitutional complaints of energy and gas companies: KGHM Polska Miedź S.A.,[33] Polskie Sieci Elektroenergety-czne S.A. (later PGE Polska Grupa Energetyczna S.A.),[34] and Rafineria Trze-binia S.A.[35] The initial lack of coherence of Constitutional Tribunal views on this issue is amply illustrated by a case concerning the first of these companies. It is worth mentioning that the legal status of KGHM Polska Miedź S.A. had changed several times. Initially, it was a state-owned enterprise (Kombinat Górniczo-Hutniczy Miedzi), then a sole-shareholder company of the State Treasury, and since 1997 it has been a listed company in which shares were held by both the State Treasury and private entities. In the judgment of May 10, 2005, Ref. No. Ts 204/04, the Constitutional Tribunal refused to proceed with its constitutional complaint arguing that KGHM was not an addressee of the freedom of economic activity, because the freedom formula did not apply to the state and its organizational forms. In the next judgment issued in this case, dated November 8, 2005, the Constitutional Tribunal granted the ap-plicant's objection and accepted the argument that due to the transformation from a sole-shareholder company of the State Treasury into a company with State Treasury shareholding, it obtained the status of an entity governed by the private law regime, and that change should justify treating the applicant as an entity that – though having its roots in the system of state institutions in the broad sense – already operated within the framework of the provisions dedicated to commercial companies. By the same token it became a holder of constitutional rights and freedoms. When the case was referred for examina-tion on the merits, in the judgment of December 20, 2007, Ref. No. SK 67/05, the Constitutional Tribunal discontinued the proceedings stating that KGHM was a public-sector economic entity, and as such, it could not hold consti-tutional rights and freedoms. The decisive argument for the Constitutional Tribunal was that the State Treasury held 41.7950% of the company's shares

---

[32] *Cf.* decisions of the Constitutional Tribunal: of December 20, 2007, Ref. No. SK 67/05; of April 8, 2008, Ref. No. SK 80/06.

[33] *Cf.* decisions of the Constitutional Tribunal: of May 10, 2005, Ref. No. Ts 203/04; of November 8, 2005, Ref. No. Ts 203/04; of May 10, 2005, Ref. No. Ts 204/04; of December 20, 2007, Ref. No. SK 67/05; of April 8, 2008, Ref. No. SK 80/06.

[34] *Cf.* decision of the Constitutional Tribunal of April, 2011, Ref. No. SK 21/07.

[35] *Cf.* decision of the Constitutional Tribunal of February 15, 2012, Ref. No. Ts 37/11.

and the state enjoyed broad powers due to the fact that the legislator treated the company as one of significant importance for the public order or public security.

The Constitutional Tribunal considered applying three different criteria in order to determine whether companies in which the State Treasury held shares were public-sector economic entities. The first one was the formal criterion, i.e. the inclusion of a given entity in the system of authorities. The Constitutional Tribunal stated that with respect to joint-stock companies in which the State Treasury held shares this could not be the decisive criterion 'in view of the changing area of the state activity, in particular the emergence of new forms in which the state pursues economic activity.'[36] The second criterion was the asset criterion, in the form of the tangible basis for the economic activity. The Constitutional Tribunal considered the criterion to be insufficient when the state's activity was based on cooperation with private capital, as is the case in 'mixed' economic entities that use both public and private assets at the same time.[37] In the latter case, the asset criterion has to be supplemented with the functional one, assuming that the public-sector status of the entity is determined from the point of view of analyzing the actual (indirect or direct) influence of state authorities on its operations.[38]

The exclusion of companies with State Treasury shareholding from the group of holders of constitutional rights and freedoms gives rise to serious doubts, as demonstrated by the dissenting opinions filed to the judgment of April 6, 2011, Ref. No. SK 21/07. In this case the full bench of the Constitutional Tribunal held that the joint-stock company Polska Grupa Energetyczna was a public-sector economic entity. When its constitutional complaint was being examined, it was a listed company, but the State Treasury held a majority block of shares (approx. 60%). In the dissenting opinions, the judges of the Constitutional Tribunal submitted, among other things, that in legal transactions a joint-stock company and its shareholders, including the State Treasury, belonged to two different categories of entities. The latter group is not permanent and, may change quickly especially when the company shares are traded on the stock exchange. Furthermore, the assets of a joint-stock company cannot be treated as the assets of individual shareholders. Regardless of whether payments for shares are made by a private or public entity, including the State Treasury, they form the single share capital of the

---

[36] Judgments of the Constitutional Tribunal: of May 7, 2001, Ref. No. K 19/00; of December 20, 2007, Ref. No. SK 67/05; of April 8, 2008, Ref. No. SK 80/06.

[37] Decision of the Constitutional Tribunal of December 20, 2007, Ref. No. SK 67/05.

[38] Decisions of the Constitutional Tribunal: of December 20, 2007, Ref. No. SK 67/05; of April 8, 2008, Ref. No. SK 80/06; of April 6, 2011, Ref. No. SK 21/07.

joint-stock company without distinguishing the parts made up of private and public funds. It is not shareholders, but company bodies, that are responsible for the day-to-day running of a joint-stock company and the regular control of its operations. Thus if a joint-stock company is a legal person separate from its shareholders, with its own assets and bodies managing its operations, its capacity to be the holder of constitutional rights and freedoms should also be assessed separately, not from the perspective of whether or not its shareholders can hold such rights and freedoms.

Chapter 3

DIRECT APPLICATION OF THE CONSTITUTION AS THE CONDITION FOR THE HORIZONTAL EFFECT OF CONSTITUTIONAL RIGHTS AND FREEDOMS

3.1. Normative Content of the Principle of Direct Application of the Constitution

The principle of direct application of the Constitution is of fundamental importance for the horizontal effect of individual's rights. It is expressed in Art. 8 para. 2 of the Polish Constitution, according to which the provisions of the Constitution shall apply directly, unless the Constitution provides otherwise. The content of this provision first raises a question about the sense of its inclusion in the fundamental law. After all, with regard to other normative acts, the Constitution as a rule does not communicate the principle of their direct application. It is assumed that, because these acts are in force, they should be applied. Moreover, the requirement of applying the Constitution is derived not only from Art. 8 para. 2 of the Constitution, but also from many other provisions thereof. According to them, the Constitution is the supreme law (Art. 8 para. 1) and a universally binding law (Art. 87 para. 1 of the Constitution), while the organs of public authority must function on the basis of, and within the limits of, the law (Art. 7 of the Constitution). Last but not least, if citizens have the duty to respect the law of the Republic of Poland (Art. 83 of the Constitution), and the Constitution itself is an element of this law, then it is included in the body of laws to which they must adhere. All of these points lead to the conclusion that the purpose of Art. 8 para. 2 of the Constitution was therefore not to prescribe that the Constitution must be applied, but to highlight that it must be applied in a special way, that is directly, unless otherwise provided therein. In connection with the foregoing there arises the question of how one should understand the concept of 'direct application of the Constitution.'

In search for the answer to this question, it is worth noting the call, in the Preamble to the Constitution, to 'all those who will apply this Constitution for the good of the Third Republic.' In this case there is no doubt that this requires a very broad interpretation of the term 'application of the Constitution,' which goes beyond the application of the law by state authorities. The adoption by the legislator of the assumption that the Constitution will be applied by 'all' allows the formulation of the thesis that private entities may also be included in this process of applying the Constitution. Furthermore, the phrase 'all those who will apply this Constitution' is clearly personalized, and it seems, should be read taking into consideration the fact that this call for the application of the Constitution comes from an entity identified in the initial part of the Preamble using the following words: 'We, the Polish Nation – all citizens of the Republic.' The call for the application of the Constitution that is made in the Preamble by 'the Polish Nation' can thus be read as being addressed not only to the state authorities, but to private entities as well.

It is worth noting that Art. 8 para. 2 of the Constitution fits into a broad formula of applying the Constitution, which is derived from the provisions of the Preamble. It is stated therein in an impersonal manner that 'The provisions of the Constitution shall apply directly, unless the Constitution provides otherwise.' Thus the application of the Constitution is not limited only to public authorities acting pursuant to the law, including the Constitution. Hence, the analysis of this provision leads to the conclusion that the Constitution does not preclude its application by private entities. Naturally, this broad understanding of the concept of the application of the Constitution will also cover the observation of its provisions. Although Art. 83 of the Constitution imposes a universal duty to observe the law, and thus also the Constitution, the same duty also rests with state authorities. It can be derived from other constitutional provisions that 'The Republic of Poland shall respect international law binding upon it' (Art. 9), MPs and Senators take an oath 'to observe the Constitution and other laws of the Republic of Poland' (Art. 104 para. 2), and when the President exercises his powers he 'shall ensure observance of the Constitution' (Art. 126 para. 2). Based on the constitutional regulations, the thesis that the application of the law refers to state authorities, while the observance of the law applies to citizens, is, at minimum, controversial.[39]

Undoubtedly, it is the courts that are the most active in the direct application of the Constitution. Hence, the concept of 'direct application' is also used in its narrow sense, specifically to describe the process in which the court de-

---

[39] When attempting to recreate the nuances in the meaning of the terms 'observing' and 'applying' the law, Z. Ziembiński came to the conclusion that 'one may speak of applying the law by state authorities and by entities which are not state authorities, if one as well as the other make use of the competences assigned to them under the competence norms.' Cf. Z. Ziembiński, "Kilka uwag o pojęciu przestrzegania i pojęciu stosowania prawa," *Państwo i Prawo*, 1 (1968), p. 11.

termines the status of an individual based on constitutional norms, which are applied either autonomously or concurrently with statutory norms. I will also address this narrow understanding of the concept of the direct application of the Constitution later in this book.

3.2. The Principle of Direct Application of the Constitution Versus the Principle of its Supremacy

The principle of direct application of the Constitution (Art. 8 para. 2) is correlated with the principle of the Constitution being the supreme law (Art. 8 para. 1). It is no coincidence that both these principles have been incorporated into a single provision.[40] Legal scholars have mentioned that both of these principles 'express the same principle of constitutionalism in its contemporary legal form and are mutually complementary.'[41] The supremacy of the Constitution inferred from Art. 8 para. 1 of the Constitution itself is expressed not only in the ban on passing normative acts that are contrary to the Constitution, but also in the imperative that the Constitution must be implemented by all the authorities of the state. The direct application of the Constitution is, in fact, an element of this latter imperative.[42] In the judgment of May 19, 1998, Ref. No. U 5/97, the Constitutional Tribunal [CT] stated: 'One of the cardinal principles of this Constitution is the principle of constitutionalism, which points to the very substance of the fundamental law by recognizing it as the supreme law of the Republic (Art. 8 para. 1). The fundamental consequence thereof is the rule that provisions of the Constitution apply directly, unless the Constitution itself provides otherwise (Art. 8 para. 2).'

The principle of direct application of the Constitution also reinforces the principle of its supremacy within the internal legal framework. Without

---

[40] A. Jamróz, "Bezpośrednie stosowanie konstytucji w kontekście jej normatywnego charakteru. Kilka refleksji" (in:) I. Bogucka, Z. Tobor (eds.), *Prawoznawstwo a praktyka stosowania prawa*, Katowice 2002, p. 141.

[41] K. Działocha, "Zasada bezpośredniego stosowania konstytucji w dziedzinie wolności i praw obywateli" (in:) *Obywatel – jego wolności i prawa: zbiór studiów przygotowanych z okazji 10. lecia urzędu Rzecznika Praw Obywatelskich*, B. Oliwa-Radzikowska, Warszawa 1998, p. 33. Likewise *cf.* P. Sarnecki, "Idee przewodnie Konstytucji Rzeczypospolitej Polskiej z 2 kwietnia 1997 r.," *Przegląd Sejmowy*, 5 (1997), p. 10; A. Chmielarz, *Funkcja prawna konstytucji na przykładzie Konstytucji Rzeczypospolitej Polskiej z 2 kwietnia 1997 roku*, Warszawa 2011, p. 184.

[42] K. Działocha, "Zasada bezpośredniego stosowania...," p. 33; L. Garlicki, "Ochrona konstytucyjności i praworządności," *Państwo i Prawo*, 10 (1987), p. 129.

the tools to directly apply the Constitution, its supremacy would be illusory. This principle also underscores the normative and binding nature of constitutional provisions.[43] However, as noted by Piotr Tuleja, the principle of the Constitution's supremacy was not always correlated with the necessity of its direct application by the courts of law.[44] In the Kelsenian model, the Constitution was only the grounds for the passing of normative acts, including statutes, and the latter were the grounds for individual decisions. It was the task of the courts of law to give statutory norms a more specific shape.

3.3. Conditions Underlying the Direct Application of the Constitution

The direct application of the Constitution by courts of law and other administrative authorities requires the fulfilment of a number of conditions.

First, the constitution needs to be a normative act containing general and abstract norms that can be the grounds for decisions applying the law, which decisions, in turn, contain individual and specific norms. This requires a departure from the concept of the constitution as a momentous and ideological document of a declarative and political nature in favor of the concept of the Constitution as an act that can be applied in practice.[45] The constitution as a normative act has no uniform nature; apart from substantive norms it also contains competence norms, program norms, or other norms, conferred with the rank of legal principles.[46] This does not alter the fact that it is normative in its entirety. Varying degrees of precision and specificity of individual provisions of the constitution do not preclude the possibility of extracting specific normative content from each of these provisions.[47]

Secondly, the direct application of the constitution, both in vertical, as well as in horizontal relations, requires that its content not be limited only to the provisions concerning the organization of the state apparatus and the

---

[43] A. Chmielarz, *Funkcja prawna konstytucji…*, p. 188.

[44] P. Tuleja, "Stosowanie Konstytucji RP przez sądy" (in:) O. Bogucki, J. Ciapała, P. Mijal (eds.), *Standardy konstytucyjne a problem władzy sądowniczej i samorządu terytorialnego*, Szczecin 2008, p. 49.

[45] K. Działocha, "Idea bezpośredniego stosowania konstytucyjnych wolności i praw" (in:) M. Jabłoński (ed.), *Wolności i prawa jednostki w Konstytucji RP*, Warszawa 2010, p. 19.

[46] P. Wronkowska, "W sprawie bezpośredniego stosowania Konstytucji," *Państwo i Prawo*, 9 (2001), p. 4.

[47] *Cf.* decision of the Constitutional Tribunal of March 22, 2000, Ref. No. P 12/98.

competences of individual public authorities, but that it also should include provisions shaping the status of an individual, both in the state and in the society. It is the constitution – not normative acts that contain more specific provisions – that should guarantee the fundamental rights and freedoms of an individual, determine his responsibilities and guarantee legal remedies. The adoption of such a concept became possible in the course of the evolution of the constitution as a normative act, from the organizational statute of the state governing the system of the state authorities and the relations between them, to a normative act also regulating the status of an individual in the state.[48]

Thirdly, the direct application of the constitution requires giving it the rank of the supreme law. It is only such a rank that determines the relations between the constitution and the other normative acts in force in the country, and thus, determines the special mode of the application of its provisions. The legal supremacy of the constitution in a negative aspect implies that sub-constitutional acts cannot contradict the constitution, while in the positive aspect, it implies that it determines the content of these acts. The problem of the legal supremacy of the constitution is of crucial importance in horizontal relations, because the latter are shaped primarily by normative acts of lower rank, the content of which is influenced by the constitution.

Fourthly, the diverse normative nature of specific constitutional provisions triggers the need to diversify the manner of their application. As stated by the Supreme Court (SC) in its judgment of March 10, 2011, Ref. No. II PK 245/10: 'Considering that the entire Constitution is to be applied in a direct way, however, it should be noted that this application will be different in the case of specific types of norms. For "self-executing" norms, a certain state of facts can be assigned to them quite easily, and the content of decisions to be taken that are based directly on the Constitution can be pointed out. In the event of other norms, such as general clauses, proceedings involving the direct application of the Constitution are more complicated. Legal content is not expressed directly in those clauses and needs to be interpreted based on the provisions of the Constitution. Thus, it is not sufficient to merely cite the wording of the fundamental law, but it becomes necessary to point to an understanding of this provision in the case law or legal studies.'

All four conditions of the direct application of the Constitution will be the subject of further deliberations. At this point, however, I would like to focus on the principle of direct application of the Constitution of the Republic of Poland expressed in its Art. 8 para. 2.

---

[48] P. Wronkowska, "W sprawie bezpośredniego...," p. 5.

3.4. Forms of Direct Application of the Constitution

The principle of direct application of the Constitution is one of the most important systemic rules of the Polish fundamental law, as demonstrated for instance by its place in the constitutional systematics. Currently, its three forms are distinguished, namely autonomous application of the Constitution, co-application of the Constitution and a statute (or another normative act) and control application.

3.4.1. Autonomous Application of the Constitution

An autonomous application of the Constitution, as indicated by legal scholars[49] and in Constitutional Court case law,[50] may take place when the constitutional provision is clear and precise and the matter regulated in it is not further elaborated, or made more specific, in a statute.

Without questioning this kind of definition of the notion of the autonomous application of the Constitution, one feels compelled to make the following reservations.

Most constitutional provisions do not meet the requirements of clarity and precision, yet this does not mean that they cannot be applied directly. It is worthwhile to observe that not only a number of constitutional provisions, but many statutory ones as well, are not unequivocal or precise. Statutory provisions abound in general clauses or indeterminate phrases. Deducing a specific and unequivocal legal norm from this kind of statutory provision often requires complex interpretation techniques. But this does not make them incapable of direct application in the courts.[51] The same conclusion

---

[49] L. Garlicki, when formulating both of these conditions for autonomous application of a constitutional norm, also added a third condition: the judge's readiness to apply a constitutional norm in such a way. L. Garlicki, "Bezpośrednie stosowanie konstytucji" (in:) *Konferencja naukowa: Konstytucja RP w praktyce (materiały z konferencji)*, Warszawa 1999, p. 24. A similar view was promoted by: W. Kręcisz, "Stanowisko sądów powszechnych wobec bezpośredniego stosowania Konstytucji," *Acta Universitatis Wratislaviensis, Przegląd Prawa Administracyjnego* LX (2004), p. 60; S. Jarosz-Żukowska, "Problem horyzontalnego stosowania…", p. 195–196.

[50] *Cf.* judgments of the Constitutional Tribunal: of March 22, 2000, Ref. No. P 12/98; of November 28, 2001, Ref. No. K 36/01.

[51] P. Kaźmierczyk provides many arguments supporting the thesis that the direct application of the constitution is independent of the unequivocal and precise formulation of its provisions. *Cf.* idem, "O bezpośrednim stosowaniu przepisów konstytucji" (in:) I. Bogucka,

should be applied to constitutional provisions. As K. Kozak says, the 'lack of clarity and general nature of the Constitution's text cannot be treated as grounds for neglecting it in building the grounds for an adjudication,' rather they should be 'the point of departure for interpretation efforts.' On the other hand, the 'clear and detailed character of the Constitution's text will depend on the circumstances in which it is applied, rather than on the way in which it is worded.'[52] Meanwhile P. Tuleja submits that in constitutional law 'the rule that the more general the provision, the smaller the possibilities of applying it, does not operate. With respect to some constitutional provisions one can identify the opposite rule. Even though provisions are formulated in a general way, one must interpret unequivocal legal norms from them. This applies first and foremost to the provisions of the Constitution that express human rights. In their case it is not the formulation that is decisive, but their function.'[53] He points out that personal rights, which serve a protective function to the greatest extent, despite being included in general constitutional provisions, cannot be regulated by statute as freely as political or social rights.[54] In addition, it should be noted that the unequivocal and specific character of a legal norm determines the margin of appreciation of the authority applying the given norm and not the very possibility of applying it. Where the norm is equivocal and not very specific, the authority has more possibilities in interpreting it, and thus, also greater freedom in applying it. But when the norm is precise and specific, the margin of appreciation of the applying authority is very narrow, while the act of applying the law is strictly determined by the norm's contents.[55] For these reasons we should state expressly that each constitutional provision, regardless of the degree of its specificity and precision, can be applied, although not necessarily autonomously.

As for the second condition of the autonomous application of constitutional provisions, i.e. the given matter not being regulated in a statute, legal scholars differ as to how it should be understood. Some believe that this is

---

Z. Tabor (eds.), *Prawo a wartości. Księga jubileuszowa Profesora Józefa Nowackiego*, Kraków 2003, p. 117–120.

[52] K. Kozak, "Konstytucja jako podstawa decyzji stosowania prawa" (in:) A. Bator (ed.), *Z zagadnień teorii i filozofii prawa*, Wrocław 1999, p. 116 et. seq. Likewise *cf.* A. Preisner, "Dookoła Wojtek. Jeszcze o bezpośrednim stosowaniu Konstytucji RP" (in:) L. Garlicki, A. Szmyt (eds.), *Sześć lat Konstytucji Rzeczypospolitej Polskiej. Doświadczenia i inspiracje*, Warszawa 2003, p. 236.

[53] P. Tuleja, "Stosowanie Konstytucji RP...," p. 59.

[54] Judgment of the Constitutional Tribunal of July 10, 2000, Ref. No. SK 12/99.

[55] These interdependencies are correctly pointed out by P. Wronkowska. *Cf.* P. Wronkowska, "W sprawie bezpośredniego...," p. 12.

a necessary condition for the autonomous application of the Constitution,[56] while others are of the opinion that the existence of a statutory regulation on a given matter does not exclude the autonomous application of the Constitution.[57] If a constitutional provision contains a reference to a statute and the latter has not been enacted, in my view, this does not make the constitutional provision incapable of autonomous application. Otherwise, the lack of a statute would deprive the constitutional provision of its attribute of applicability, which would be contrary to Art. 8 para. 2 of the Constitution. Thus, the application of the Constitution cannot depend on a statute being enacted.[58] On the other hand, if a constitutional provision does not contain a reference to statutory law, this does not prevent it from being further elaborated through a relevant statutory regulation. Such a possibility would be excluded only if the statutory norm were limited to repeating the contents of the constitutional norm which could not be further elaborated or made more specific in any way. This is precisely the character of constitutional norms that enshrine the generally applicable and absolute prohibition of interference with the sphere of an individual's freedom.[59] Constitutional norms such as the prohibition of torture or of forcing anyone to disclose their beliefs can only be applied autonomously.

Beyond any doubt, situations in which the court bases the adjudication solely on a constitutional provision that is applied autonomously are exceptional and rare.[60] As the Constitutional Tribunal held in its judgment of March 22, 2000, Ref. No. P 12/98: 'since in our legal order there are very few matters in which constitutional norms have not been made more specific or further elaborated in ordinary legislation, the process of direct application of the Constitution usually has the form of co-application of a constitutional

---

[56] B. Nita, "Bezpośrednie stosowanie konstytucji a rola sądów w ochronie konstytucyjności prawa," *Państwo i Prawo*, 9 (2002), p. 38; A. Wasilewski, "Przedstawianie pytań prawnych Trybunałowi Konstytucyjnemu przez sądy (art. 193 Konstytucji)," *Państwo i Prawo*, 8 (1999), p. 28.

[57] P. Sarnecki, "Stosowanie Konstytucji PRL w orzecznictwie Naczelnego Sądu Administracyjnego," *Studia Prawnicze*, 3 (1988), p. 62; P. Czarny, B. Naleziński, "Bezpośrednie stosowanie konstytucji; normy samowykonalne w konstytucji" (in:) J. Trzciński (ed.), *Charakter i struktura norm konstytucji*, Warszawa 1997, p. 133; A. Mączyński, "Bezpośrednie stosowanie konstytucji przez sądy," *Państwo i Prawo*, 5 (2000), p. 6; K. Działocha, "Stosowanie Konstytucji PRL," *Acta Universitatis Nicolai Copernici. Prawo XXIV*, 156 (1985), p. 19; B. Banaszak, "Prawa człowieka i obywatela w nowej Konstytucji Rzeczypospolitej Polskiej," *Przegląd Sejmowy*, 5 (1997), p. 62.

[58] A. Bałaban, "Źródła prawa w polskiej konstytucji z 2 kwietnia 1997 r.," *Przegląd Sejmowy*, 5 (1997), p. 39.

[59] P. Wronkowska, "W sprawie bezpośredniego...," p. 14.

[60] P. Tuleja, "Stosowanie Konstytucji RP...," p. 54.

norm (principle) and the relevant statutory norms.' Nevertheless the Constitutional Tribunal does not rule out autonomous application of the Constitution in some cases.[61]

In case law, the autonomous application has often concerned Art. 45 of the Constitution when statutory provisions did not foresee the initiation of court proceedings in a given case.[62] By way of an example, we can mention the resolution dated January 6, 2005, Ref. No. III CZP 75/2004, in which the Supreme Court [SC] stated that an association member's claim for the protection of his membership against removal from the association, in contravention of the law or charter, could be examined in court. It should be explained that in the Act – Law on Associations[63] there is no provision that grants members of an associations the possibility of bring a claim in order to protect their membership before a court. But the Supreme Court held that 'the right of court access is a subjective right, giving the grounds for an individual's claim, and by virtue of Art. 8 para. 2 of the Constitution, it can provide autonomous legal grounds for the relevant claim. Being "everyone's" right, regardless of the existence and contents of the substantive law relation, it means that the individual can oblige the relevant state authorities (courts) to take measures provided for in statutory law and needed in order to issue a judgment in a case which was not excluded from the judicial path by statute.'

In case law there is a prevailing view that it is impossible to autonomously apply general constitutional principles, such as the principles of freedom or equality. In a judgment dated May 9, 2003, Ref. No. V CK 344/2002, the Supreme Court held that Art. 31 paras. 1 and 2 of the Constitution could not be applied by courts as autonomous grounds for resolving cases. The principle of the freedom of a person that it expresses is, according to the Supreme Court, 'a general clause defining the method and direction of interpretation of the whole system of constitutional norms, while courts can directly apply as autonomous grounds for resolving a case only those provisions of the Constitution which are formulated precisely enough that they can be referred to specific situations.' Yet in the judgment of February 8, 2012, Ref. No. I SA/Kr 2059/11, the Provincial Administrative Court in Kraków ruled: 'The principle of equality before the law, enshrined in Art. 32 of the Constitution, is a general clause and cannot be autonomous, substantive-law grounds for an adjudication.' An identical standpoint was expressed by the Supreme Court

---

[61] *Cf.* judgment of the Constitutional Tribunal of May 19, 1998, Ref. No. U 5/97.

[62] *Cf.* resolution of the Supreme Court of January 18, 2001, Ref. No. III ZP 28/00.

[63] Act of April 7, 1989 – Law on Associations, Official Journal of Laws (Dz. U.) of 2001, No. 79, item 855, as amended.

in the judgment dated March 14, 2002, Ref. No. III RN 141/2001, in which it held: 'Art. 32 of the Constitution, which contains a declaration of equality of all people before the law and their equal treatment by public authorities, as well as a prohibition of discrimination in political, social or economic life, for whatever reason, does not constitute grounds for a claim which might be effectively pursued before an authority appointed to do so.' I fully share the view that it is impossible to autonomously apply the Constitution's general principles, because of their purposefully indeterminate character, which makes it impossible to resolve specific court cases on the basis of principles such as the principles of freedom or equality alone.

3.4.2. Co-application of the Constitution and Statutes

The co-application of provisions of the Constitution and of statutes occurs when a given matter is regulated at the level of the Constitution and statutes at the same time. Then, as the Constitutional Tribunal accepts in its case law, 'a constitutional provision either – alongside the statutory provision – becomes the material for building a legal norm (which is only possible when that provision is sufficiently specific and precise), or determines the manner of establishing the legal meaning of the statutory provision (which takes the form of the so-called statutory interpretation consistent with the Constitution and may also be done on the basis of general constitutional principles).' [64] It should be noted that the co-application of the Constitution and a statute should take into account the different manners and scopes of regulating the given matter in each of those normative acts. Thus, the direct application of the Constitution need not mean exactly the same thing as the direct application of a statute,[65] even though both these acts can be applied in parallel as the legal grounds for adjudication in particular cases. Constitutional provisions are formulated in more general terms, while statutory provisions are usually specific and precise. Therefore, the former will be applied differently from the latter, although applying them together must be regarded as a form of the direct application of the Constitution to which Art. 8 para. 2 refers.

The co-application of the Constitution and statutes may have an ornamental, interpretative or modifying character.[66]

---

[64] Judgment of the Constitutional Tribunal of November 28, 2001, Ref. No. K 36/01.

[65] *Cf.* P. Kaźmierczyk, "O bezpośrednim stosowaniu…," p. 116 and 118.

[66] L. Garlicki, "Bezpośrednie stosowanie konstytucji," p. 24; W. Kręcisz, "Stanowisko sądów powszechnych…," p. 66–67; P. Waldziński, "Stosowanie Konstytucji w orzecznictwie

The ornamental co-application of the Constitution and statutes occurs when a statutory provision constitutes the proper legal grounds for the adjudication, while a constitutional provision is only quoted as a supporting argument or as a confirmation of the correct direction of interpretation. In this case, the statutory provision is clear, specific and does not arouse constitutional doubts, so the constitutional provision can hardly be seen as co-forming, in any way, the legal grounds for the court's adjudication. This type of co-application of the Constitution and statutes receives various assessments in the legal literature. Leszek Garlicki draws attention to its educational value, stressing that it is worthwhile 'to promote it, because it will help overcome the psychological resistance against using the Constitution in other cases, when it may indeed be necessary.'[67] On the other hand, Wojciech Kręcisz believes that this kind of co-application of the Constitution is 'in essence "empty" and is not relevant for adjudicating on the merits of the case.'[68]

The interpretative co-application of the Constitution and statutes occurs when the constitutional provision determines the manner which the statutory provision is understood and applied. The actual legal grounds for adjudication are found in the statutory provision, the contents of which are determined by implementing the technique of interpreting it in accordance with the Constitution.[69] This form of co-application plays a particular role when the application of the directives of linguistic interpretation to a statutory provision does not permit a single, clearly determined meaning to be ascribed to it. In such a situation, interpreting a provision consistently with the Constitution makes it possible to choose, from among the alternative meanings, the one that, to the highest degree, takes into account constitutional norms, principles and values. Interpreting a statute in accordance with the Constitution may involve either finding an understanding of the provision that makes it consistent with constitutional values to the greatest extent (the intensive model) or excluding an understanding of the provision that would make it contrary to those values (the extensive model).[70] As the Constitutional Tribunal held in its judgment of June 14, 2004, Ref. No. P 17/03, 'all authorities applying the law have a duty to interpret the provisions they apply consistently with the Constitution and – where different interpretation conclusions are possible – choose the solution which is the closest to the constitutional

sądowym" (in:) D. Dudek, A. Janicka, W.P. Staszewski (eds.), *Ius et Veritap. Księga poświęcona pamięci Michała Staszewicza*, Lublin 2003, p. 372.

[67] L. Garlicki, "Bezpośrednie stosowanie konstytucji," p. 25.

[68] W. Kręcisz, "Stanowisko sądów powszechnych...," p. 67.

[69] P. Tuleja, "Stosowanie Konstytucji RP...," p. 55.

[70] Ibidem.

text, principles and values. At the same time it is necessary to reject an interpretation which leads to conclusions contrary to these criteria. This is, among other things, a sign of operationalization of Art. 8 para. 2 of the Constitution ("The provisions of the Constitution shall apply directly, unless the Constitution provides otherwise") with respect to public authorities, to which courts belong.[71]

The third type of co-application of the Constitution and statutes is referred to as modifying co-application.[72] The aim of a modifying co-application is to 'rescue' the constitutionality of a statutory provision by ascribing a meaning to it that makes it consistent with the Constitution. In this way, the understanding of a provision is modified, compared with the understanding determined on the basis of traditional interpretation methods. An interpretation consistent with the Constitution cannot, in principle, overcome the unequivocal results of linguistic interpretation, but, in my opinion, one important exception to the rule must be allowed. If the meaning of the provision that is determined by the directives of linguistic interpretation is contrary to the constitutional system of values, the provision should be ascribed contents that will preserve the axiological coherence of the law. However, with respect to modifying co-application, an objection is sometimes raised – and it clearly is not unfounded – that it has a law-making character, and it allows the retention of a provision in the legal system that, at first sight, appears to be unconstitutional.

3.4.3. Control Application of the Constitution and Statutes

The control application of the Constitution occurs in cases involving a conflict between a constitutional provision and a statutory or lower-ranking provision, when the conflict makes it impossible to apply both provisions and cannot be resolved by an interpretation consistent with the Constitution. A constitutional provision is then used as a model for the review of another provision. It cannot, however, act as an independent derogation force if an inconsistency is found between it and that other provision, which is also an

---

[71] The Constitutional Tribunal expressed the same view in its judgment of October 27, 2004, Ref. No. SK 1/04.

[72] Some perceive modifying co-application as a kind of interpretative co-application. *Cf.* L. Garlicki, "Bezpośrednie stosowanie konstytucji", p. 15. However others express criticism of modifying co-application. *Cf.* T. Zieliński, in: *Konferencja naukowa: Konstytucja RP w praktyce (materiały z konferencji)*, Warszawa 1999, p. 34; A. Jamróz, "Bezpośrednie stosowanie…", p. 156.

element of the binding legal order. If a sub-statutory provision is found to be unconstitutional, the court can omit it while resolving a case, but if a statutory provision is found unconstitutional, a legal question has to be submitted to the Constitutional Tribunal in order to initiate a procedure that is aimed at depriving the provision of its binding force. The courts are bound by the statutes in force (Art. 178 para. 1 of the Constitution), regardless of whether they conform to the Constitution or not.

In the Supreme Court case law, the problem of the direct application of the Constitution has, for a long time, been considered mainly in the context of potential conflicts between statutes and the Constitution. The controversies concerned the question whether a court, upon finding a statute unconstitutional, could refuse to apply it and base the adjudication on the Constitution alone or whether it had a duty to submit a legal question to the Constitutional Tribunal, and once the statute had been repealed, consider an adjudication based on a constitutional norm.[73] At the Supreme Court – Labor Law, Social Insurance and Public Affairs Chamber, the dominant view has been that, if a court has any doubts about the constitutionality of a statutory provision, it has no duty to submit a legal question to the Constitutional Tribunal, but could refuse to apply that provision.[74] In the case law of the Supreme Court – Civil Chamber, there have been major discrepancies on the issue. Sometimes, the Supreme Court has excluded the possibility for a court to refuse to apply a statutory provision that was considered unconstitutional,[75] but on other occasions, it has conceded that a court did have such a power.[76]

Currently, the dominant view in the case law is that a court cannot ignore a statutory provision that it considers to be unconstitutional. In this respect, a representative judgment was issued on April 2, 2009, Ref. No. IV CSK 485/2008. The Supreme Court held in it that the principle of direct application, expressed in Art. 8 para. 2 of the Constitution entails the court's

---

[73] *Cf.* e.g. resolution of the Supreme Court of September 20, 1988, Ref. No. III AZP 14/87 and judgments of the Supreme Court: of May 14, 1996, Ref. No. III ARN 93/95; of April 7, 1998, Ref. No. I PKN 90/98; of May 26, 1998, Ref. No. III SW 1/98; of June 20, 2000, Ref. No. I KZP 14/00; of September 26, 2000, Ref. No. III CKN 1089/00; of July 4, 2001, Ref. No. III ZP 12/01.

[74] *Cf.* e.g. judgments of the Supreme Court: of May 14, 1996, Ref. No. III ARN 93/95; of August 29, 2001, Ref. No. III RN 189/00; decision of the Supreme Court of May 26, 1998, Ref. No. III SW 1/98.

[75] *Cf.* e.g. judgments of the Supreme Court: of September 18, 2002, Ref. No. III CKN 326/01; of October 30, 2002, Ref. No. V CKN 145/00; of November 21, 2003, Ref. No. I CK 323/02; of April 16, 2004, Ref. No. I CK 291/03.

[76] *Cf.* e.g. judgments of the Supreme Court: of September 26, 2000, Ref. No. III CKN 1089/00; of August 25, 2003, Ref. No. V CK 47/02.

duty to adjudicate in line with the priorities set forth in the Constitution. In other words, the courts have a duty to engage in pro-constitutional interpretation, but they have no power to declare a provision unconstitutional and to remove it from the legal system. If they have doubts as to the conformity of a provision with the Constitution, they should submit a legal question to the Constitutional Tribunal.

However, some legal scholars[77] and judges[78] believe that a court may refuse to apply a statutory provision that is obviously incompatible with the Constitution. In line with this view, the duty to submit a legal question to the Constitutional Tribunal would only apply in dubious cases, which require considerable expert knowledge and institutional authority.[79] The problem also arises with respect to statutory provisions that are outside of the scope of the Constitutional Tribunal jurisdiction, such as provisions that have lost their binding force and statutory provisions whose content is identical to that of provisions that have already been held unconstitutional. In this case, it is permissible for the courts to ignore them, because their unconstitutionality has been established, and there is no competition between the powers of the court and the Constitutional Tribunal.[80]

3.5. Exceptions to the Rule of Direct Application of the Constitution

Pursuant to Art. 8 para. 2 of the Constitution, its provisions are applied directly, unless it provides otherwise. This provision suggests that there may be various ways of applying the Constitution, with direct application being only one of them. Another conclusion is that the direct application of the Constitution is a principle for which exceptions may be specified within the constitutional provisions. Yet, those exceptions do not mean that some constitutional provisions are not applicable, but rather, that they are to be applied in a way other than directly. However, an analysis of the constitutional pro-

---

[77] K. Kolasiński, "Zaskarżalność ustaw w drodze pytań prawnych do Trybunału Konstytucyjnego," *Państwo i Prawo*, 9 (2001), p. 31; R. Hauser, "Zapytajcie Trybunał," *Rzeczpospolita*, March 18, 2002; A. Preisner, *Dookoła Wojtek. Jeszcze o bezpośrednim...*, p. 241–242

[78] *Cf.* judgment of the Supreme Administrative Court of October 24, 2000, Ref. No. V SA 613/00.

[79] A. Preisner, "Dookoła Wojtek. Jeszcze o bezpośrednim...," p. 241–242.

[80] *Cf.* judgments of the Supreme Court: of January 20, 2004, Ref. No. IV KK 434/03, of October 9, 2001, Ref. No. IV KKN 328/97.

visions gives rise to serious doubts about whether the 'Constitution provides otherwise', i.e. regarding another way to apply its provisions.[81]

The conclusion, from an analysis of the materials documenting the work of the National Assembly's Constitutional Commission, is that the circumstances that were mentioned the most often as an exception to the principle of direct application involved a constitutional regulation that required further elaboration or concretization in a statute, that became the legal grounds for adjudication. An alternative to the direct application of the Constitution was intended to be its application 'via' a statute. Thus, the direct application of the Constitution was seen as synonymous with its autonomous application, i.e. applying its provisions as if there was no 'intermediary' statute.[82]

The current understanding of the notion of the direct application of the Constitution, as presented above, differs considerably from the view dominant until 1997. The direct application of the Constitution is understood as covering not only its autonomous application, but also its co-application with a statute or another normative act. With such a broad notion of the direct application of the Constitution, one should draw the conclusion that it is not an exception to the principle of direct application of the Constitution when a constitutional matter is further elaborated or clarified by an 'intermediary' statute. The application of the latter, together with the Constitution, is also a form of the direct application of the Constitution. Thus, we can consider that the view equating the direct application with the autonomous application of the Constitution, that is, without the 'intermediation' of a statute, is no longer valid. The lack of statutory regulation is not a necessary condition for all forms of the direct application of the Constitution, but only for its autonomous application.

---

[81] More on the subject, *cf.* M. Florczak-Wątor, "Wątpliwości dotyczące wyjątku od zasady bezpośredniego stosowania Konstytucji RP," *Zagadnienia Sądownictwa Konstytucyjnego*, 2 (2012), p. 7–21.

[82] On the subject of the meaning of the notion of an 'intermediary' statute, *cf.* P. Wronkowska, "W sprawie bezpośredniego…," p. 9–10.

Chapter 4

THE SCOPE OF THE HORIZONTAL EFFECT
OF CONSTITUTIONAL RIGHTS

4.1. Preliminary Remarks

Acceptance of the approach according to which constitutional rights may have a horizontal dimension raises a question of the extent of their influence upon relations between private entities. The essence of this type of relations lies in both the parties being the beneficiaries of constitutional rights; hence, both the parties may invoke these rights demanding respect and protection for them. In the event of a collision of constitutional rights, it is necessary to delineate the scope of the horizontal effect of each of those rights, so that they can be exercised by both the right holders to the greatest extent possible. The idea of the scope of the horizontal effect of constitutional rights under the Polish law is most generally expressed in Art. 31 para. 2 of the Constitution, which imposes upon everyone an obligation to respect the freedoms and rights of others. At the same time, the successive paragraph of this Article grants to the legislator the right to interfere into horizontal relations in order to restrain constitutional rights of one entity in order to protect constitutional rights of another entity. Eventually, it is therefore the legislator, and then the court, that determines the scope of the horizontal effect of constitutional rights. The former will do so in an abstract manner and the latter in a tangible manner, taking into account the merits of the examined case.[83] The purpose of this chapter is to describe the most optimum mechanism that would allow distinguishing, on an abstract and concrete planes, the constitutional rights that remain in a collision in horizontal relations.

---

[83] Similar view was promoted by: A. Barak, "Constitutional human rights...," p. 265; W. Voermans, "Applicability of fundamental rights in private law: What is the legislature to do? An intermezzo from a constitutional point of view" (in:) T. Barkhuysen, P.D. Lindenbergh (eds.), *Constitutionalisation of Private Law*, Leiden 2006, p. 36–37.

4.2. The Notion of Collision of Constitutional Rights

Collision of constitutional rights is a phenomenon which is inscribed in the very heart of their existence. Two constitutional rights vested in two different entities driven by the desire to pursue their own, often opposing, interests inevitably trigger a collision. The legislator is far from attempting to prevent a collision of constitutional rights; quite the contrary – it attempts to describe and regulate it as one of many circumstances that simply occur in social life.

Collision is defined as a concurrence of something that is incompatible or conflicting with something else, a clash of a moving object with another object, or simply a dispute, conflict or feud.[84] Therefore, when referring to a collision of constitutional rights, we mean such circumstances when there is a 'clash' of these rights, their confluence, conflict or when a full exercise of these rights is unviable due to the restrictive impact occurring between the conflicting rights. Collision of constitutional rights may have an abstract dimension, when we examine it at the level of legal norms, their binding scope and application, or a tangible dimension, when we consider it in the context of a clearly defined state of facts, wherein the said collision has occurred or could occur. We can thus abstractly ponder the problem of collision between two rights, for instance between the right to privacy and the right to public information. Under these circumstances, we will seek to establish the extent of the binding force and application of these rights, and to delineate their overlapping scope, where collision could occur. We may also consider the problem of collision between the same constitutional rights *in concreto*, for instance when a journalist intends to publish information relating to a private life of a public official against the latter's desire, and thus a collision, which needs to be resolved, occurs between the right to public information and the right to privacy.

From the point of view of the mechanism for resolving a collision between constitutional rights, it is important to distinguish between an actual collision, which in the later part of this work I would name an actual collision, and its imaginary existence, which I will call an abstract collision. The legislator refers to the latter while laying down the principles of resolving collisions of constitutional rights, guided by its notion and the anticipated likelihood of its occurrence. In turn, courts rule on a collision of constitutional rights *in concreto*, that is when such a collision does in fact occur. It is so, since the

---

[84] *Cf. Słownik języka polskiego* PWN, http://sjp.pwn.pl; P. Żmigrodzki (ed.), *Wielki słownik języka polskiego*, http://wsjp. pl.

legislator acts prophylactically to prevent a collision, while a court passes its ruling subsequently and repressively.

4.3. Constitutional Rights as Principles (Optimization Requirements)

Analyzing the problem of collision of constitutional rights requires looking at these rights from the point of view of a division, almost universally approved by legal scholars, into principles and rules.[85] Although different criteria of such a division are advocated, the most important ones seem to be the criterion of generality[86] and the criterion of the degree of compliance, required for their execution.[87] Principles are norms with a high degree of generality; moreover, they are optimization requirements that can be satisfied to varying degrees. In contrast, rules are norms with a lower degree of generality which are always either fulfilled or not. Compliance with rules to a certain extent only is not possible.

The difference between principles and rules is reflected in the very method of resolving collisions occurring between them. In the event of a conflict between two rules, the only valid solution is to apply one of those rules and to refuse to apply the other. Two rules with mutually exclusive contents cannot be concurrently applied. Robert Alexy explains that a conflict between rules can be resolved by either introducing into one of the rules a clause with an exception that will remove the conflict or by excluding one of the rules from the system.[88] Deciding which of the rules will apply requires adoption of specific collision rules. On the other hand, in the event of a collision between principles, the aim is to attain the fullest possible implementation of each of them, whereas the principle which is granted precedence restricts the implementation of the opposing principle. Thus, finding a collision between two

---

[85] R. Alexy, *Theorie der Grundrechte…*, p. 71 et. seq.; T. Gizbert-Studnicki, "Zasady i reguły prawne," *Państwo i Prawo*, 3 (1988); P. Tuleja, *Normatywna treść praw jednostki w ustawach konstytucyjnych RP*, Warszawa 1997, p. 68 et. seq.; M. Novak, "Three models of balancing (in constitutional review)," *Ratio Juris*, 1 (2010), p. 101; R. Alexy, "Rights and liberties as concepts" (in:) M. Rosenfeld, A. Sajó (eds.), *The Oxford Handbook of Comparative Constitutional Law*, Oxford 2013, p. 291–297; K. Wojtyczek, *Sądownictwo konstytucyjne w Polsce. Wybrane zagadnienia*, Warszawa 2013, p. 34–35.

[86] *Cf.* R. Alexy, *Theorie der Grundrechte…*, p. 73 and the German sources stated therein.

[87] Ibidem, p. 75–76.

[88] Ibidem, p. 77.

principles being on a par level does not lead to the inference that one of them is not applicable, but requires establishing a relation of precedence between them against the background of the circumstances that caused the collision.[89]

An example of principles embodying optimization requirements are constitutional norms that express certain rights or freedoms.[90] Rules are an exception amongst such norms; they occur when the norm introduces a right that is absolute in nature.[91] Such a right cannot be subject to restrictions, thus it can be exercised either fully or not at all.[92] The category of rules in the Polish Constitution includes norms prohibiting violation of person's dignity (Article 30),[93] norms prohibiting torture or cruel, inhuman, or degrading treatment or punishment (Article 40) or the ban imposed upon public authorities to compel anyone to disclose his philosophy of life, religious convictions or belief (Article 53 para. 7). As remarked by R. Alexy, when applying these norms, it is not their precedence that is being taken into account, but the fact whether they can be violated.[94]

Except for absolute rights, all other constitutional rights may be realized not only fully, but also to a certain degree. Hence, norms expressing these constitutional rights are, according to the theory by R. Alexy, principles that can stand in a collision against each other. They are therefore optimization requirements that should be realized to the greatest extent possible. Such a view on constitutional rights as principles (optimization requirements) leads to

---

[89] P. Tuleja, *Normatywna treść praw...*, p. 72.

[90] R. Alexy, "Discourse theory and fundamental rights" (in:) A.J. Menedez, E.O. Eriksen (eds.) *Arguing Fundamental Rights*, Dordrecht 2006, p. 23; A. Barak, *Proportionality. Constitutional Rights and Their Limitations*, Cambridge 2012, p. 39; M. Novak, "Three models of balancing...," p. 101; P. Tuleja, *Normatywna treść praw...*, p. 128–129. In a ruling of January 31, 2013, Ref. No. K 14/11, the Constitutional Tribunal found that 'some constitutional norms have the features of principles expressing orders or optimization requirements, and that collisions between these principles may be resolved only on the basis of the principle of proportionality.'

[91] For reference on absolute rights, *cf.* A. Barak, *Proportionality. Constitutional Rights...*, p. 27–32; M. Klatt, M. Meister, *The Constitutional Structure of Proportionality*, Oxford 2012, p. 29–42; B. Cali, "Balancing human rights? Methodological problems with weights, scales and proportions," *Human Rights Quarterly*, 29 (2007), p. 258.

[92] The mechanism of balancing values underlying absolute rights is thus not applicable for the purpose of protecting these rights, since these rights cannot be exercised to a certain degree only. *Cf.* M. Klatt, M. Meister, *The Constitutional Structure...*, p. 29. A different view is promoted by A. Barak who claims that the principle of proportionality can be applied for both principles as well as rules. *Cf.* A. Barak, *Proportionality. Constitutional Rights...*, p. 6.

[93] *Cf.* judgment of the Constitutional Tribunal of September 30, 2008, Ref. No. K 44/07 on permission to shoot down of a civilian aircraft used as a weapon of terrorist attack.

[94] For reference on absolute nature of human dignity, *cf.* R. Alexy, *Theorie der Grundrechte...*, p. 95–96; A. Barak, *Proportionality. Constitutional Rights...*, p. 28.

the conclusion that, on the one hand, they protect the interests of certain entities and, on the other hand, they express values which the constitutional legislator considered treasured and worthy of protection. This is precisely how the individual and universal aspect of constitutional rights is manifested. The collision between constitutional rights is in practice the collision between the interests of these rights' beneficiaries and the values underlying them, since neither the interests nor the values can be fully realized while in collision. This type of collision cannot be resolved by assuming that one of the constitutional rights is not applicable or, as an exception, that it may remain unapplied. This would mean that the interests of certain entities and values underlying certain constitutional rights would be deprived of protection contrary to the provisions of the Constitution. Therefore, when resolving a collision between constitutional rights, in each and every case a conditioned precedence should be established with an aim to apply both these rights within the limit as determined by the said precedence.[95]

4.4. The Principle of Proportionality and Its Importance for the Horizontal Effect of Constitutional Rights

Resolving a collision between constitutional principles by establishing the conditioned precedence requires, according to the theory by R. Alexy,[96] applying the so-called proportionality test. Most often the principle of proportionality is considered the principle that sets the limits of state interference into the sphere of individual's rights, that is, the principle operating in vertical relations. As stated by K. Wojtyczek, in this sense the principle of proportionality is a 'general principle binding upon state authorities in all the cases

---

[95] Such an approach to the manner of resolving collisions of constitutional rights can be found in the case law of the Constitutional Tribunal. In its judgment of March 20, 2006, Ref. No. K 17/05, the Constitutional Tribunal stated: 'First of all, a collision of rights and principles at a constitutional level may not eventually lead to a full elimination of one of the conflicting rights. The problem that needs to be resolved in such a case always involves finding a certain point of equilibrium, balancing the values protected under the Constitution and delimiting the application of each of the rights. Secondly, in such a case (the case of conflicting rights), the existing basic axiological preferences are always of essential importance; such preferences may be decoded based on the analysis of values regarded as guiding or supreme at the level of the general principles of the Constitution.'

[96] R. Alexy, "Constitutional rights, balancing, and rationality," *Ratio Juris*, 16 (2003), p. 135; R. Alexy, "Balancing, constitutional review, and representation," *International Journal of Constitutional Law*, 3 (2005), p. 572.

of their competences of power, including legislative powers, where specific legal regulations leave some decision-making margin, that is, the ability to choose between alternative ways of action.[97] Such is the origin of this principle which, when introduced into the German legal system at the end of the 19th century, was originally targeted at public administration and was later deployed in the jurisprudence of the Federal Constitutional Court as a principle binding upon the legislator.[98] The judgment of the Federal Constitutional Court of 1958 on the *Lüth* case is pointed to in the German legal literature as the first cardinal decision that applied the balancing mechanism and at the same time founded the doctrine of indirect horizontal effect of constitutional rights.[99] At present, the principle of proportionality is applied in most countries of Western Europe and in the jurisprudence of the European Court of Human Rights and the Court of Justice of the European Union.[100]

It has also been adopted under the German law and is now generally accepted[101] that the principle of proportionality comprises three specific sub-principles.[102] The first of these is the sub-principle of adequacy, which

---

[97] For reference on the legislator's freedom to apply the principle of proportionality, *cf.* A. Barak, "Proportionality" (in:) M. Rosenfeld, A. Sajó (eds.), *The Oxford Handbook of Comparative Constitutional Law*, Oxford 2013, p. 247–248.

[98] For reference on origins of this principle, *cf.* J. Bomhoff, *Balancing Constitutional Rights. The Origins and Meanings of Postwar Legal Discourse*, Cambridge 2013, p. 28 et. seq.; B. Schlink, "Proportionality" (in:) M. Rosenfeld, A. Sajó (eds.), *The Oxford Handbook of Comparative Constitutional Law...*, p. 728–729; K. Wojtyczek, *Granice ingerencji ustawodawczej w sferę praw człowieka w Konstytucji RP*, Kraków 1999, p. 140.

[99] J. Bomhoff, *Balancing Constitutional...*, p. 128.

[100] A. Stone Sweet, J. Mathews, "Proportionality balancing and global constitutionalism," *Columbia Journal of Transnational Law*, 47 (2008), p. 97–159; M. Cohen-Eliya, I. Porat, "The hidden foreign law debate in Heller: The proportionality approach in American Constitutional Law," *San Diego Law Review* 46 (2009), p. 369 and 381; M. Cohen-Eliya, I. Porat, "Proportionality and the culture of justification," *The American Journal of Comparative Law* 59 (2011), p. 464; M. Klatt, M. Meister, *The Constitutional Structure...*, p. 2–3; J. Bomhoff, *Balancing Constitutional Rights ...*, p. 11.

[101] R. Alexy, "Constitutional rights, balancing,...," p. 135; R. Alexy, "Balancing, constitutional review...," p. 572; A. Stone Sweet, J. Mathews, "Proportionality balancing...," p. 75; M. Cohen-Eliya, I. Porat, "The hidden foreign law...," p. 380; M. Cohen-Eliya, I. Porat, "Proportionality and the culture...," p. 464; P. Greer, "'Balancing' and the European Court of Human Rights: a Contribution to the Habermas – Alexy debate," *Cambridge Law Journal*, 63 (2004), p. 415–416; M. Kumm, "Who is afraid of the total constitution? Constitutional rights as principle and the constitutionalization of private law," *German Law Journal*, 4 (2006), p. 348; A. Barak, *Proportionality. Constitutional Rights...*, p. 3; M. Klatt, M. Meister, *The Constitutional Structure...*, p. 8; B. Schlink, "Proportionality," p. 722–725; K. Möller, *The Global Model of Constitutional Rights*, Oxford 2012, p. 181.

[102] These three elements of proportionality express the idea of optimization, since constitutional rights as principles are in fact optimization requirements. Besides these, the rational end

prescribes that when limiting the rights of an individual driven by the need to achieve certain ends, the state should choose such measures that will be suitable to effectively achieve the set aims. Another sub-principle, i.e., the principle of necessity, requires the state to choose, amongst various means capable of obtaining the desired end, the one which is the least burdensome for an individual. Last but not least, the principle of proportionality *stricto sensu*, which is the third sub-principle, prescribes the need to maintain an appropriate proportion between the chosen means and the desired end. It requires deployment of a mechanism for reaching a balance between the goods in collision, that is, the goods that have been affected by the undertaken measures and the goods which the state aims to protect via its interference.[103] The balancing process defined in such a way, as stated by R. Alexy, is a special method of applying principles understood as optimization requirements.[104] The requirements of adequacy and necessity permit determining the scope of realization of the given principle under certain factual circumstances. Whether a measure of interference with constitutional rights is adequate in terms of achieving a desired end and whether it is not unduly burdensome for an individual can only be determined in consideration of the facts. On the other hand, the requirements of proportionality *stricto sensu* and purposefulness of the interference are formulated in the normative sphere and analyzed there as well.[105]

In the Polish legal system, the principle of proportionality was formulated in the case law of the Constitutional Tribunal during the early 1990s, that is, based on the provisions of the former Constitution. This principle, originally termed non-excessive state interference in the rights of an individual, has been inferred by the Constitutional Tribunal from the principle of protecting

---

to be achieved is distinguished as a separate element of the proportionality test. *Cf.* M. Klatt, M. Meister, *The Constitutional Structure...*, p. 8.

[103] As stated by L. Garlicki, 'The principle of proportionality expresses the belief that the degree of intensity of interference with the legal status of an individual must find its justification in the status of the public interest which is promoted in this manner.' *Cf. ibidem*, note no. 28 re. art. 31 para. 3 of the Constitution (in:) L. Garlicki (ed.), *Konstytucja Rzeczypospolitej Polskiej. Komentarz*, Warszawa 2002, p. 28. Likewise K. Wojtyczek, *Granice ingerencji ustawodawczej...*, p. 159; M. Cohen-Eliya, I. Porat, "Proportionality and the culture...," p. 464.

[104] R. Alexy, "Rights and liberties...," p. 291; R. Alexy, "Discourse theory and fundamental...," p. 23. Jurisprudence also mentions the balancing (weighting) mechanism as one of the methods of interpreting the text of the constitution. *Cf.* T.A. Balmer, K. Thomas, "In the balance: Thoughts on balancing and alternative approaches in state constitutional interpretation," *Albany Law Review*, 75 (2012–2013), p. 2037; T. Lenckner, "The principle of interest balancing as a general basis of justification," *Brigham Young University Law Review*, 1986, p. 653.

[105] R. Alexy, "Discourse theory and fundamental...," p. 23; M. Klatt, M. Meister, *The Constitutional Structure...*, p. 10.

citizens' trust in the state and its laws.[106] In the Constitution of the Republic of Poland currently in force, the principle of proportionality is expressed in Art. 31 para. 3, according to which limitation upon the exercise of constitutional freedoms and rights may be imposed by the legislator only when 'necessary' in a democratic state for the protection of values enumerated in the said provision.[107] In one of its first rulings issued after the Constitution came into force, i.e., the judgment of June 9, 1998, Ref. No. K 28/97, the Tribunal held that 'the requirement of "necessity" is met if the imposed restrictions are consistent with the principle of proportionality.' The principle of proportionality is also expressed in Art. 228 para. 5 of the Polish Constitution, according to which actions undertaken by the state as a result of the introduction of any extraordinary measure must be proportionate to the degree of threat. Last but not least, this principle is embraced in two specific limitation clauses contained in Art. 51 para. 2 and Art. 53 para. 5 of the Polish Constitution, which lay down the requirement of 'necessity' ('indispensability') of the introduction by the legislator of limitations upon the right to protection of personal data and the freedom to manifest one's religion. Thus, there is no doubt that all the references to the principle of proportionality expressed in the text of the Polish Constitution point to the possibility of its application in vertical relations between an individual and the state, while Art. 31 para. 3, Art. 51 para. 2, and Art. 53 para. 5 of the Polish Constitution correlate this principle with the legislator's actions, and finally Art. 228 para. 5 of the Polish Constitution correlates it with any actions by a public authority taken as a result of the introduction of an extraordinary measure.

The principle of proportionality may, however, be contemplated also in a completely different dimension than the aforementioned vertical dimension, namely when the party that interferes with the constitutional rights is not a state, but a private entity.[108] This does not mean a legal obligation for private entities to apply the principle of proportionality for the purpose of taking action relating to other private entities. In their mutual relations, private entities are not guided by constitutional values, but their own values, which

---

[106] *Cf.* judgments of the Constitutional Tribunal: of January 26, 1993, Ref. No. U.10/92; of June 26, 1995, Ref. No. K 11/94; Ref. No. K 12/93; Ref. No. K 9/95.

[107] The source of the principle of proportionality continues to be also the principle of a democratic state ruled by law expressed in Art. 2 of the Constitution.

[108] A. Stone Sweet, J. Mathews, "Proportionality balancing and global…," p. 73; M. Tushnet, "An essay on rights," *Texas Law Review*, 8 (1984), p. 1373; P. Greer, "'Balancing' and the European Court…," p. 412; L. Fastrich, "Human rights and private law" (in:) K.P. Ziegler (ed.), *Human Rights and Private Law. Privacy as Autonomy*, Oregon 2007, p. 30.

they respect and pursue in their actions.[109] Meanwhile, the use of balancing mechanism[110] is possible only in reference to a relatively consistent axiology, such as the one derived from the constitution. Accordingly, this mechanism cannot be employed once there is a collision of two different axiological systems without any common denominator.

The principle of proportionality will therefore be applied in horizontal relations not by private individuals, but by the state that resolves disputes between private entities, taking into consideration constitutional axiology. The obligation of a preventive (or, one should rather say, prophylactic) application of this principle rests with the legislator that regulates these horizontal relations,[111] while the obligation of its repressive application rests with courts that resolve disputes arising between private entities as a result of collision of their constitutional rights. Thus, it should be inferred that the principle of proportionality determines the scope of the horizontal effect of constitutional rights. Two of its component elements, that is, the principles of necessity and adequacy, are targeted directly at the legislator and set the limits of statutory interference with horizontal relations. It clearly arises under these two principles that the state can interfere with relations between private entities only when such interference is adequate to achieve the desired end, applying means that are necessary, yet at the same time also the least intrusive. The objective to justify the state's interference in horizontal relations may involve both the need to protect constitutional rights of one of the parties to this relation (restoring a disturbed balance

---

[109] It is also pointed to by G.C.N. Webber. *Cf. idem*, "Proportionality, balancing, and the cult of constitutional rights scholarship," *Canadian Journal of Law and Jurisprudence*, 1 (2010), p. 193.

[110] In jurisprudence, attention is drawn to existence of doubts as to the object that is being balanced, namely whether these are values, rights or interests. *Cf.* e.g. M. Klatt, M. Meister, *The Constitutional Structure…*, p. 16 et. seq.; T.A. Aleinikoff, "Constitutional law in the age of balancing," *The Yale Law Journal*, 96 (1987), p. 945. In further considerations, I favor the view that it is the values underlying constitutional rights in collision or goods of public nature that are being balanced. In other words, a collision that occurs at the level of constitutional rights must be resolved at their underlying foundations, and thus by way of balancing the values that justify the existence and protection of certain constitutional rights. Needless to say, this means that axiology is involved in the balancing mechanism, yet there is no doubt that the balancing mechanism may not be detached from axiological aspects, regardless of what is being balanced. *Cf.* M. Klatt, M. Meister, *The Constitutional Structure…*, p. 52.

[111] Looking for balance between competitive values involves putting forward a question about the society we live in and the values that are respected in this society. The legislator is accountable to that society (the electorate), thus it seems that it has a stronger mandate than a court to resolve a conflict of values. *Cf.* A. Barak, *Proportionality. Constitutional Rights…*, p. 90; N. Petersen, "How to compare the length of lines to the weight of stones: Balancing and the resolution of value conflicts in constitutional law," *German Law Journal*, 14 (2013), p. 1393.

between the parties), as well as protection of a public good (such as order or public security). On the other hand, the principle of proportionality *stricto sensu* determines the manner of state interference in horizontal relations, advocating that the state cannot deprive a single entity in such relations of its constitutional rights in order to facilitate the application of another entity's constitutional rights, and that it must balance the viability of applying both these constitutional rights.[112] Therefore, the application of the principle of proportionality *stricto sensu* by the state requires considering the degree to which the values underlying one constitutional right may be sacrificed in order to facilitate the application, also to a certain extent, of the values underlying a different constitutional right.[113] Values underlying constitutional rights are first balanced by the legislator by way of establishing the conditioned precedence, and then by the court by way of passing judgements, with due consideration for statutory regulations, on disputes between private entities.[114]

Admissibility of applying the principle of proportionality not only in vertical, but in horizontal relations as well, is confirmed by the analysis of values underlying the admissible restrictions upon constitutional rights and freedoms. It is worth noting that Art. 31 para. 3 of the Polish Constitution clearly differentiates between two types of values with regard to which the legislator may restrict the exercise of constitutional rights and freedoms of an individual. The first type are values of a public nature, such as security or public order, protection of the natural environment, health or public morals. Due to the need of protecting those values, the state limits the individual's rights primarily in vertical relations. Freedoms and rights of others comprise a different type of values, the need to protect which may justify the statutory limitation of constitutional rights and freedoms of an individual. In this case, the rights and freedoms of both the parties to horizontal relations are subject

---

[112] This idea is expressed in the German jurisprudence in the 'Praktische Konkordanze' concept by Konrad Hesse. For more reference on this concept, *cf.* T. Marauhn, N. Ruppel, "Balancing conflicting human rights: Konrad Hesse's notion of „Praktische Konkordanz" and the German Federal Constitutional Court" (in:) E. Brems (ed.), *Conflicts Between Fundamental Rights*, Antwerp 2008, p. 279 et. seq.

[113] According to R. Alexy, the 'balancing law' which is a part of the proportionality test, can be expressed as a law, according to which the higher the degree of non-fulfillment or impairment of one principle, the greater must be the importance of the fulfillment of the other principle. *Cf.* R. Alexy, *Theorie der Grundrechte…*, p. 146; R. Alexy, "Discourse theory and fundamental…," p. 23.

[114] Likewise *cf.* A. Barak, "Constitutional human rights…," p. 265; W. Voermans, "Applicability of fundamental rights…," Leiden 2006, p. 36–37.

to balancing.[115] On the one hand, these are constitutional rights and freedoms which are limited, while on the other hand, all rights and freedoms, regardless of their legal status, need to be protected and this justifies the legislator's interference.

Application of the principle of proportionality in horizontal relations gives rise to problems that do not arise when this principle is applied in vertical relations.[116] In horizontal relations, the legal status of the two entities is identical in the sense that both are the beneficiaries of constitutional rights and freedoms that need to be protected by the state. The problem therefore lies not in determining the conditions of one entity's interference with a constitutional right of another entity, but in determining the scope of the necessary protection of both the entities' constitutional rights. This kind of problem does not occur when the principle of proportionality is applied in vertical relations. The state is regarded as a violator of those constitutional rights, of which it is not the beneficiary. Thus, what is balanced here is a value of a public nature that justifies state interference, such as order or public security, and the value underlying the limited constitutional rights of an individual. State interference in constitutional rights of an individual must be justified based on the applicable law. In turn, interference of an individual with constitutional rights of another individual is tantamount to exercise of freedom and personal autonomy by the former. The task of the state is to merely delimit the exercise of this freedom, so that other individuals are free to benefit from their freedoms as well. Absence of such limits means that an individual needs not justify his interference with the rights of another individual otherwise than by reference to the exercise of his own rights.

---

[115] Naturally the horizontal relation may be not only two-party, but multi-party as well, yet it has no major significance from the point of view of the described mechanism of balancing the values underlying constitutional rights.

[116] *Cf.* R. Alexy, *Theorie der Grundrechte…*, p. 480; A.R. Madry, "State action and the obligation of the states to prevent private harm: the Rehnquisttransformation and the betrayal of fundamental commitments," *Southern California Law Review*, 65 (1992), p. 840.

4.5. The Mechanism of Balancing Values Underlying Constitutional Rights

4.5.1. The Notion of Values

The balancing mechanism applied in horizontal relations therefore focuses on values underlying constitutional rights.[117] What it involves is a qualitative comparison of the values in collision rather than their quantitative comparison, hence the notions of balancing or weighing are merely metaphors that do not accurately reflect actions taken with respect to conflicting values. A close and inextricable relationship connects constitutional rights and the values underlying these rights.[118] On the one hand, values as well as rights can remain in collision that needs to be resolved by establishing a relation of conditioned precedence. On the other hand, a progressive exercise of constitutional rights, which according to the theory by R. Alexy, are principles (optimization requirements), corresponds with a gradual implementation of values underlying these rights. Constitutional rights always have certain axiological grounds. The values underlying these rights determine the relation of precedence between them, and thus are a necessary component of the aforementioned balancing mechanism.

In order to determine what this value balancing mechanism is, we need, in the first place, to define two key notions, namely the notion of 'values' and the notion of a 'system (order) of values.' As regards the first of these notions, it is most often treated as the primary and indefinable notion, and if an attempt to explain its meaning is made, then it is most often designated with the use of a combination of various descriptors, for instance 'that what is valuable, being desired, calls for implementation, fulfils the needs, etc.'[119] It is highlighted that value is a feature (attribute) of preciousness of an object, item, phenomenon, speech, etc. assigned to it based on assessments formed

---

[117] B. Schlink, "Proportionality...," p. 724; J.M. Shaman, *Constitutional Interpretation. Illusion and Reality*, Westport 2001, p. 44; K. Möller, *The Global Model...*, p. 99.

[118] R. Alexy, *Theorie der Grundrechte...*, p. 125–126. As stated by Z. Kędzia, based on the civil-law theory of values, 'civil rights proclaim and protect a set of values that unite a community organized into a state. In other words, these rights are the drivers of a progressive integration process, which in turn is the essence of social life.' Cf. idem, "Horyzontalne działanie praw obywatelskich" (in:) J. Łętowski (ed.), *Państwo, prawo, obywatel*, Wrocław–Warszawa–Kraków–Gdańsk–Łódź 1989, p. 523.

[119] M. Kordela, *Zarys typologii uzasadnień aksjologicznych w orzecznictwie Trybunału Konstytucyjnego*, Poznań 2001, p. 25.

in a given social environment. Preciousness is expressed in the totality of appreciative judgments.[120] Z. Ziembiński assumes that value lies in 'that what is sufficiently permanently approved by the given entity'.[121] Not always, however, the notion of value is related to the requirement of approval of a specific state of affairs. On the contrary, S. Wronkowska states: 'If a similar method of evaluating certain states of affairs emerges in any social group, it is said that these states of affairs are considered values by this group'.[122] M. Kordela cultivates a similar approach: 'Value is the state of affairs approved or disapproved (or treated in an indifferent way) by a specific entity'.[123]

A set of ordered values is termed a value system.[124] For further considerations, the value system underlying the legal system is of essential importance.[125] The relationship between norms and values is expressed in the statement that 'norms assume values, since what they demand aims at giving effect to values'.[126] The purpose of a legal norm which is an utterance of a prescriptive nature is to protect the values underlying the said norm. The content of legal norms permits not only articulating protected values, but also determining relations occurring between them, including their preference as to their priority. A certain strategy for attaining and protecting certain values is also encoded in the legal system, which the legislator sets for the addressees of these norms, obliging them to implement it. Values in turn rationalize legal norms, legitimize them and form the criteria for their evaluation.[127] For these reasons, it should be deemed that each norm belonging to the legal system has specific axiological grounds,[128] while the foundation underlying these norms is a certain set of values. The axiological foundation of the law must be consistent and coherent, whilst its constituent values cannot be mutually exclusive.

---

[120] H. Groszyk, L. Leszczyński, "Wartości pozaprawne w procesie stosowania klauzul generalnych" (in:) H. Rot (ed.), *Problemy metodologii i filozofii prawa*, Wrocław 1988.

[121] Z. Ziembiński, *Wartości konstytucyjne. Zarys problematyki*, Warszawa 1993, p. 12.

[122] Z. Wronkowska, *Podstawowe pojęcia prawa i prawoznawstwa*, Poznań 2005, p. 191.

[123] M. Kordela, *Zarys typologii…*, p. 28.

[124] P. Wronkowska, *Podstawowe pojęcia prawa…*, p. 191.

[125] K. Pałecki, "Wstęp" (in:) K. Pałecki (ed.), *Dynamika wartości w prawie*, Kraków 1997, p. 9.

[126] P. Dutkiewicz, *Problem aksjologicznych podstaw prawa we współczesnej polskiej filozofii i teorii prawa*, Kraków 1996, p. 33. H. Groszyk and L. Leszczyński are of an opinion that drafting normative acts with due regard for values involves formulating evaluative statements (expressing values) in a form of coded phrases in the language of the law. *Cf.* H. Groszyk, L. Leszczyński, "Wartości pozaprawne…"

[127] K. Pałecki, "Wstęp"…, p. 8.

[128] M. Kordela, *Zarys typologii…*, p. 29

In the legal literature, a dispute is pending as to whether values exist objectively and can be the subject of cognition, or perhaps are merely a reflection of judgements by a specific individual, all while being inexistent in the objective sense.[129] According to this second approach, values comprise certain ideal and desirable states of affairs and need not find reflection in any tangible objects. Solution of this problem, which is the subject of a dispute between supporters of axiological cognitivism and axiological non-cognitivism, goes far beyond the scope of this book. However, determining the mode in which values exist does not seem essential from the point of view of an aspect that is more significant for further considerations, namely the distinction between internal values of law and extralegal values.[130] The first are incorporated into the legal system by the legislator, while the latter are not expressed in the text of legal provisions, yet are not always indifferent for the legislator. In both these cases, these values may comprise values existing objectively beyond the legal system as well as values being a reflection of the judgments that have not been expressed in the content of legislative provisions. There may be varying reasons why certain values remain beyond the legal system. Some of these values are seen by the legislator as less important and hence left out beyond the scope of legal regulation, while other are not incorporated into the legal system due to difficulties in their formulation. By changing the law, the legislator can also change the nature of particular values, either incorporating them into, or excluding them from, the legal system. On the other hand, change of values constituting the axiological foundations of the legal system can prompt a change in the manner of interpreting a legal provision, whilst its wording remains unchanged. It is a process which also works the other way round, i.e., absence of change in the axiological foundations limits the room for an effective introduction of normative changes, since provisions in their new wording will be interpreted in line with their 'old spirit.'[131] In this context, the necessity of mutual adjustment of norms and values is often mentioned.[132] The axiological foundation of law cannot be, as rightly pointed out by Krzysztof Pałecki, 'imposed by a decree. It is a "product" of a complex process of shaped beliefs, stabilization of attitudes, formation of ideals and ideologies and their internalization.'[133]

---

[129] P. Dutkiewicz, *Problem aksjologicznych podstaw…*, p. 69–70; M. Kordela, *Zarys typologii…*, p. 25–26.

[130] J. Kaczor, "Z problematyki klauzul generalnych w Konstytucji RP" (in:) A. Bator (ed.), *Z zagadnień teorii i filozofii prawa. Konstytucja*, Wrocław 1999, p. 160.

[131] K. Pałecki, "Wstęp…," p. 11.

[132] Ibidem, p. 12.

[133] K. Pałecki, *Zmiany w aksjologicznych podstawach prawa jako wskaźnik jego tranzycji* (in:) K. Pałecki (ed.), *Dynamika wartości w prawie*, Kraków 1997, p. 27.

4.5.2. Axiological Foundations of the Constitution

A system of values underlying the legal system of a given country finds its reflection in the constitution as the supreme law of that country.[134] According to Piotr Winczorek, nowadays 'adoption of a constitution (...) is not possible without an explicit or implicit reference to some set of values.'[135] With this assumption as a starting point for further considerations, it is worth noting that the axiology of the constitution could be analyzed in two dimensions.[136] First of all, the constitution is a value in itself, regardless of the specific solutions adopted in its text, and this is due to the function it fulfils in a society and the state. Secondly, specific solutions adopted in the constitution are based on certain axiological assumptions and reflect specific axiological choices made by the constitutional legislator.[137]

As mentioned by Z. Kędzia, the word 'constitution' means a 'special social order formed by ethical norms, the way of organizing community life, which prevents autocracy, ensures a proper conduct of overall affairs, guarantees freedom of an individual; last but not least creates frames for the social integration processes. It is expected of a written constitution that it will be a normative basis for such a social order, for such an organization of community life.'[138] This ability to set order and organize the affairs of the state and the society allows assuming that every constitution is a value in itself, regardless of the specific solutions adopted in its content.

At the core of each constitution lie certain values by which its drafters were driven when accepting the existing and not any other solutions. The axiology of the constitution defines its tangible identity. The list of fundamental values on which the Constitution is based is as a rule contained in its preamble. Recreating the comprehensive axiology of the constitution requires, however, taking into account all the constitutional provisions that either directly or indirectly express the idea of protecting specific values.

---

[134] P. Wronkowska, *Podstawowe pojęcia prawa…*, p. 191; A. Niżnik-Mucha, „Kilka refleksji na temat wartości konstytucyjnych w świetle założeń pozytywizacji praw człowieka," *Przegląd Prawa Gospodarczego*, 7–8 (2010), p. 8.

[135] P. Winczorek, *Dyskusje konstytucyjne*, Warszawa 1996, p. 117.

[136] A two-dimensional view on constitutional axiology was earlier presented by Z. Kędzia. *Cf.* idem, *Uwagi o aksjologii konstytucji* (in:) A. Rzepliński (ed.), *Prawa człowieka w społeczeństwie obywatelskim*, Warszawa 1993.

[137] It must be emphasized that constitutional values are not created by the constitutional legislator, but are recognized by it as those which are subject to protection under the constitution. *Cf.* H. Nieuwenhuis, "Fundamental rights talk…," p. 4.

[138] Z. Kędzia, "Uwagi o aksjologii…," p. 24–25. Similar view was promoted by P. Dutkiewicz. *Cf.* idem, *Problem aksjologicznych podstaw…*, p. 97.

Every constitution should express a more or less coherent axiological system.[139] Even if one should have doubts as to whether specific values belong to this system or as to their importance and place in the hierarchy of this system, it is not possible to undermine the argument that such an axiomatic system exists at all.[140] In its juridical decisions, the Federal Constitutional Court had repeatedly fostered a view that the constitution incorporates the so-called objective system (order) of values, which means that the values expressed through its provisions take the form of objective principles, recognized by the constitutional legislator as being worthy of protection, and therefore esteemed and promoted. References to the Constitution of the Republic of Poland as the source of the objective system (order) of values can also be found in juridical decisions of the Constitutional Tribunal. For the first time, reference to the conception of an objective system of values was made by judge L. Garlicki in a dissenting opinion to the judgment of the Constitutional Tribunal of May 28, 1997, Ref. No. K 26/96, concerning the conditions for permissibility of abortion. He stated that 'an objective system of values resulting from the totality of norms and constitutional principles imposes upon us a duty to treat conceived life as autonomous legal good which is entitled to constitutional protection.' Two years later, the notion of an objective system of values appeared in the Constitutional Tribunal judgment of March 23, 1999, Ref. No, K 2/98, concerning a ban on sale of pharmaceuticals and medical materials in the absence of the possibility to register the turnover in these pharmaceuticals and materials with cash registers. The Constitutional Tribunal proclaimed then: 'The totality of the provisions of the constitution reflects a certain objective system of values, which is to be given effect through the process of interpretation and applying various constitutional provisions. (...) Since (...) certain objective system of values is derived from the constitution, then it is the legislator's duty to pass laws with such content, so as to allow for the protection and implementation of these values to the widest extent possible.' This view was then reiterated by the Constitutional Tribunal in its judgment of October 8, 2002, Ref. No. K 36/00, concerning the constitution-

---

[139] L. Garlicki, "Aksjologiczne podstawy reinterpretacji konstytucji" (in:) M. Zubik (ed.), *Dwadzieścia lat transformacji ustrojowej w Polsce*, Warszawa 2010, p. 90; P. Tuleja, *Normatywna treść praw...*, p. 90–91.

[140] As regards doubts in this regard, *cf.* K. Wojtyczek, *Sądownictwo konstytucyjne...*, p. 60. The author states that in practice the 'imprecise and fragmented constitutional axiology must be passed through the prism of subjective beliefs of members of the bodies that apply the Constitution. Within the limits set by the text of the Constitution and the accepted principles of interpretation and legal argumentation, each of these persons reads out and determines the axiology of this normative act in accordance with his own system of values.'

ality of the provisions governing the professional status of a policeman, and in its judgment of July 9, 2009, Ref. No. SK 48/05, concerning the obligation to wear seat belts in motor vehicles. In all these judgments, the Constitutional Tribunal invoked the notion of the 'objective system of values,' which is of fundamental importance for the conception of the indirect horizontal effect of constitutional rights adopted by the German Federal Constitutional Court. It should be added that, in addition to the notion of 'objective system of values,' also the notion of 'objective order of values' appeared in the case law of the Constitutional Tribunal. In its judgment of July 8, 2008, Ref. No. P 36/07, the Constitutional Tribunal stated that 'the Constitution (...) creates an objective order of values.' It should be recognized that both these notions are synonymous, since there are no grounds to assume the Constitutional Tribunal applies them in any other sense. Juridical statements in which the Constitutional Tribunal uses the phrase 'order of values and constitutional principles' should be treated likewise.[141] A more general reference to this idea is to be found in the judgment of September 30, 2008, Ref. No. K 44/07, concerning the constitutionality of the provision permitting the shooting down of a civilian aircraft used as a weapon of terrorist attack. The Constitutional Tribunal stated in this judgment that nowadays the law is understood 'not only as a set of provisions laid down in accordance with a formally defined procedure, but as a composition of axiologically and teleologically related norms, being a cultural product rooted in the historical heritage of the community and built based on a system of values common for a given group of entities.'

Resolving a collision of constitutional rights by delving into their axiological foundations requires not only establishing that those axiological grounds are an element of a certain coherent system (order) of constitutional values, but also that this system (order) exhibits relative stability and durability. It is a necessary prerequisite for endowing the resolutions for collisions of constitutional rights with the attributes of at least minimal predictability and certainty. Correlating this requirement with the axiological system of the Constitution of the Republic of Poland, we must note that formally it does not contain the so-called unamendable provisions that may not be repealed or modified. Nonetheless, its Preamble contains a call upon 'all those who will apply this Constitution for the good of the Third Republic' to respect these principles 'as the unshakeable foundation of the Republic of Poland.' In this case, the term 'principles' could be regarded as synonymous with the notion of 'values' employed in the earlier part of the Preamble. The fact that these

---

[141] L. Garlicki, "Aksjologiczne podstawy reinterpretacji konstytucji...," p. 90. Likewise P. Tuleja, *Normatywna treść praw...*, p. 90–91.

values constitute the 'foundation' – and an 'unshakeable' one at that – of the state should be regarded as a call for stabilization of the constitutional system of values in such a shape that has been endowed to it by the Constitution. This is not meant to imply that any changes, particularly singular, in that system of values are absolutely banned. The Preamble does not venture that far to claim that constitutional principles are an unshakeable foundation of the Republic of Poland, but merely calls upon all those who will apply the Constitution to respect these principles 'as the unshakeable foundation of the Republic of Poland.' Nonetheless, such wording employed in the Preamble testifies to the fact that the legislator intended to emphasize the significance of durability and stability of the constitutional system of values.

Besides the above-mentioned attributes, the constitutional system of values should, however, be also flexible so as to prevent it from fossilization and going out of date. Attainment of this flexibility is possible thanks to open conceptions in the constitution, the contents of which can be determined by reference to the extralegal system only, such as 'human dignity', 'freedom', 'justice' or 'the common good.' As mentioned by L. Garlicki, 'even if these notions gradually gain a normative content (are positivized) in the constitutional case law, their sense and original meaning lie in the non-constitutional (not to say supra-constitutional) sphere.'[142] The text of the constitution therefore allows to recreate the axiological system existing beyond this text, adopted by the constitutional legislator for its purposes. Reference to the specific values in the text of the constitution may either be direct or indirect.[143] In the first case, the values are expressed and named directly in the constitution, while in the latter case, they can be reconstructed from the constitutional provisions which envisage the protection of certain rights, goods or interests.

4.5.3. Axiology of Constitutional Rights and Freedoms of an Individual

The catalogue of constitutional rights and freedoms should be based on legible axiological foundations underlying the concept of constitutional regulation.[144] When construing constitutional provisions, the legislator can either rely on the existing axiological system, for example the system of Christian values, or a system of universal values approved and promoted by interna-

---

[142] L. Garlicki, "Aksjologiczne podstawy reinterpretacji...," p. 102.
[143] Z. Kędzia, "Uwagi o aksjologii...," p. 27.
[144] Ibidem, p. 30.

tional law, or attempt to mirror a system of values functioning in a pluralistic society that accepts the conditions of its existence *hic et nunc*.[145] It is also possible to combine these axiological systems to the extent such systems are not conflicting with each other.

The axiology of constitutional rights and freedoms of an individual is not, however, limited to the sum total of values underlying individual rights and freedoms. It also embraces mutual relations between these values; therefore, we can talk of an orderly axiological system. Decoding individual constitutional values is just as important as the reconstruction of this system of mutual correlations and ties, so that collisions of values in specific circumstances may be resolved. Although it is not possible to define a hierarchy of constitutional values *in abstracto*,[146] yet the recognition of values in the constitution allows us to reconstruct the precedence of some of them over the other. There is no doubt that in the Polish legal system, like in the legal systems of many other countries, human dignity is the cardinal value in the constitution.[147] As found by the Constitutional Tribunal in its judgment of September 30, 2008, Ref. No. K 44/07, 'the notion of human dignity should be ascribed the attribute of a constitutional value of central importance for building axiology of the current constitutional solutions.' The elements that bind this axiological system into a single coherent whole are also the other keynotes enshrined in the constitution, such as freedom or equality. Axiological preferences of the constitutional legislator can also be expressed in the schematic order of the constitution, namely the order of regulating constitutional rights and their arrangement under the various chapters. Differentiating the manner and procedures for amending constitutional provisions is of similar importance, particularly that in the event of change in the content of constitutional rights under Chapter II of the Polish Constitution, it is possible to seek a decision of the sovereign to be expressed in a referendum. Another expression of specific axiological preference is the exclusion of the possibility to limit, on less restrictive conditions, some of the constitutional rights in the event of an extraordinary measure.[148]

At the same time, the above-mentioned principle of protection of and respect for human dignity sets the limits for the mechanism of balancing

---

[145] Likewise *cf.* P. Dutkiewicz, *Problem aksjologicznych podstaw...*, p. 99.

[146] T. Lenckner, "The Principle of interest...," p. 651.

[147] B. Banaszak, "Ogólne wiadomości o prawach człowieka" (in:) B. Banaszak, A. Preisner, *Prawa i wolności obywatelskie w Konstytucji RP*, Warszawa 2002, p. 91; A. Niżnik-Mucha, "Kilka refleksji na temat...," p. 15.

[148] A. Niżnik-Mucha, "Kilka refleksji na temat...," p. 15.

the values underlying constitutional rights.[149] Constitutional rights which have their source in a person's dignity cannot be limited to a point where this dignity is violated. When balancing the values underlying the constitutional rights, the legislator, and subsequently a court, should strive to ensure that the dignity of each party to a horizontal relation was protected in equal measure. Protection afforded to constitutional rights in fact derives from the protection afforded to human dignity. In other words, constitutional rights need to be protected precisely because they are a form of expressing human dignity. The more a constitutional right is associated with dignity, the lesser the consent for limiting this right.

4.5.4. Principles of the Value Balancing Mechanism

These considerations lead to the conclusion that collision of constitutional rights is resolved at the level of their axiological foundations. This process involves establishing to what extent the right which has precedence due to a greater importance of its axiological foundations may limit the other right, and to what extent this other right cannot be limited due to the need to protect its own axiological foundations. It is therefore not possible to resolve the collision of constitutional rights by an analysis carried out at the level of colliding rights, both of which have the same status and enjoy the same protection. The Constitutional Tribunal has aptly pointed this out in its judgment of March 20, 2006, Ref. No. K 17/05, relating to limiting the protection of the right to privacy of persons holding public functions. The Constitutional Tribunal stated then that 'each of the rights enjoying constitutional guarantees, i.e., the right to privacy and the right of access to information, can in terms of proportionality be treated as the basis for delineating the scope of interference with the other right: given such an assumption, the right to privacy will therefore create a barrier against interference with the sphere of the right to information, while the right to information will, conversely, justify interference with the sphere of the right to privacy. At this level of analysis, it is therefore not possible to balance the emerging collision of rights.'

Thus, collision of constitutional rights needs to be resolved at the level of their axiological foundations, and this in turn, apart from defining the values underlying the specific constitutional rights, necessitates determining

---

[149] H. Nieuwenhuis, "Fundamental rights talk...," p. 5.

their importance (weight) and the precedence relationship between them.[150] The condition for determining the precedence relation involves adopting an assumption according to which the constitutional system of values exhibits certain characteristics of a hierarchical order.[151] These are certain types of axiological preferences that can be decoded from the text of the Constitution and that facilitate the 'presumption of protection precedence' of certain constitutional rights over and above other rights.[152]

Determining the relation of conditioned precedence is in the first place the task of the legislator, who based on constitutional axiology defines the scope of protection of constitutional rights in the event of a collision.[153] In other words, the legislator specifies the conditions under which one of constitutional rights will take precedence over the other right, and will thus restrain the other right. It is the legislator that introduces a limit on one right for the sake of protecting the other. It is also the legislator's duty to ensure that the substance of any of these rights will not be violated while resolving their collision, and that their limitations will be proportionate. In this respect, the nature of the legislator's interference is preventive (prophylactic) and abstract. Its preventive (prophylactic) attribute does not mean that once collision circumstances are regulated by the legislator, it would prevent the reoccurrence of these circumstances in the future. It does, however, mean that before an actual collision of rights occurs, the principles permitting its resolution will be laid down by the legislator in advance. The abstract attribute means, in turn, that the legislator imposes certain principles of resolving collisions of constitutional rights that constitute some sort of a model to

---

[150] R. Alexy pointed out that balancing of values underlying constitutional rights is a process that comprises three distinguishable stages. Under the first stage, the degree of non-satisfaction of the first right, in other words of the sacrificing of the first right is established. Then, the importance (degree of weight) of satisfying the competing right is established. Finally, in the third stage, the degree to which the importance of satisfying the latter right justifies the non-satisfaction of the former right is determined.' Cf. R. Alexy, "Balancing, constitutional review...," p. 574; R. Alexy, "Discourse theory and fundamental...," p. 25. Likewise cf. M. Klatt, M. Meister, *The Constitutional Structure...*, p. 10.

[151] As stated by K. Wojtyczek, 'resolving the collision of constitutional principles for the purposes of applying the Constitution requires determining the importance of specific values and their place in the constitutional hierarchy of valuep.' K. Wojtyczek, *Sądownictwo konstytucyjne...*, p. 60.

[152] Cf. judgment of the Constitutional Tribunal of October 30, 2006, Ref. No. P 10/06.

[153] Constitutional provisions serve as a 'manual' for the legislator as to how to implement fundamental rights in relations between private entities. Based on this, the legislator incorporates guidance in the private law for courts regarding interpretation and application of private law with due consideration for fundamental rights. Cf. W. Voermans, "Applicability of fundamental rights...," p. 36–37.

be applied by courts to the facts of a specific case. It is so, since a specific collision of constitutional rights, namely a collision that would actually occur, will be resolved by courts bound in this regard by the framework or guidelines of the legislator. A problem arises when such framework or guidelines are lacking, while the court faces the necessity to resolve a collision of constitutional rights based on the constitution, in accordance with the principle of its direct application.[154] Under these circumstances, there is a problem of the court's legitimacy to balance constitutional values in an abstract way and to lay down the principles for resolving the collision of constitutional rights.[155] In accordance with the principle of division of powers, decisions of this type are reserved for the parliament endowed with the democratic mandate to make the law, granted to it by the people in an electoral process. In the absence of a legislator's decision in this regard, in my opinion, it should only be acceptable for courts alone to resolve collisions of constitutional rights in exceptional cases, namely when the application by the court of the balancing mechanism in the event of a collision of constitutional values would give a clear and undisputable outcome.

The above-described mechanism of balancing values underlying constitutional rights finds its application both to resolve collisions within the sphere of negative or positive rights, as well as to resolve collisions occurring between these two types of rights. The latter situation occurs when one party enjoys negative rights that require the state to refrain from interference, while the other party of the same legal relations enjoys positive rights requiring the state to take positive action.[156]

Special importance of the above-described mechanism of balancing collisions of constitutional rights is emphasized in the modern jurisprudence and case law of many states. It is said that constitutional law 'entered the balancing era'[157] and that the balancing mechanism is one of the elements that define the modern constitutionalism.[158] It should be noted, however, that the approach

---

[154] It is mentioned in the jurisprudence that in the event of absence of statutory guidance, the burden of balancing the values underlying constitutional right rests with judges, whose decisions take on political features in this regard. Cf. P. Laing, D. Visser, "Principles, policy and practice: Human rights and the law of contract" (in:) E. Reid, D. Visser (eds.), *Private Law and Human Rights. Bringing Rights Home in Scotland and South Africa*, Edinburgh 2013, p. 334.

[155] A. Stone Sweet, J. Mathews, "Proportionality balancing...," p. 87; T.M. Scanlon, "Adjusting rights and balancing values," *Fordham Law Review*, 72 (2004), p. 1478.

[156] M. Klatt, M. Meister, *The Constitutional Structure...*, p. 86 et. seq.

[157] T.A. Aleinikoff, "Constitutional law in the age...," p. 943; G.C.N. Webber, "Proportionality, balancing...," p. 179; J. Bomhoff, *Balancing Constitutional Rights...*, p. 12.

[158] A. Stone Sweet, J. Mathews, "Proportionality balancing...," p. 74; M. Cohen-Eliya, I. Porat, "The hidden foreign law...," p. 369; M. Klatt, M. Meister, *The Constitutional Structure...*,

to understanding and applying the balancing mechanism can be different in individual countries, hence all sorts of generalizations should be approached carefully.[159]

The mechanism of balancing values underlying constitutional rights is on the one hand commonly accepted and applied in a number of countries, and on the other hand, criticized by certain legal scholars.[160] Opponents of this mechanism put forward arguments that it is based on intuition and improvisation and lacks rational elements, precision and consistency in designing the balancing criteria. Consequently, similar cases are resolved in a different manner, thus revealing its arbitrary nature. Establishing a balance between principles in collision requires finding their common denominator, whilst it does not exist.[161] It is also not possible to establish a hierarchy of these principles in an abstract way. In response to these arguments, A. Barak points out that such a common denominator is the social significance of the exercise of one right at the expense of another right or public interest.[162] In turn, T.A.Aleinikoff notes that the only problem is that of selecting an appropriate comparative scale that would permit finding a common denominator for these values, whereas the scale of values must be objective in nature and independent of personal preferences of individual judges.[163] The rationality of the balancing mechanism originates from the motivation approach applied within the framework of this mechanism, whilst a certain margin of freedom

---

p. 1; J. Bomhoff, *Balancing Constitutional Rights...*, p. 12; R. Alexy, "Discourse theory and fundamental...," p. 23.

[159] For similarities and differences in applying the mechanism of balancing in different legal systems, *cf.* J. Bomhoff, "Balancing, the global and the local: Judicial balancing as a problematic topic in comparative (constitutional) law," *Hastings International and Comparative Law Review*, 31 (2008), p. 555 et. seq.; A. Stone Sweet, J. Mathews, "Proportionality balancing...," p. 77–78; M. Cohen-Eliya, I. Porat, "The hidden foreign law...," p. 405–408; J. Bomhoff, *Balancing Constitutional Rights...*, p. 28 et. seq.

[160] For arguments in favor of and against applying this mechanism, *cf.* A. Barak, *Proportionality...*, p. 457 et. seq.; A. Barak, "Proportionality," p. 749–751; M. Klatt, M. Meister, *The Constitutional Structure...*, p. 1–4; R. Alexy, "Constitutional rights, balancing and rationality...," p. 134 et. seq.; R. Alexy, "Discourse theory and fundamental...," p. 24–25; N. Petersen, "How to compare the length...," p. 1387 et. seq.; T.A. Aleinikoff, "Constitutional law in the age...," p. 972 et. seq.; M. Tushnet, "An essay on rights...," p. 1371–1375; P. Greer, "'Balancing' and the European...," p. 414 et. seq.; F. Du Bois, "Rights trumped? Balancing in constitutional adjudication," *Acta Juridica*, 2004, p. 157 et. seq.

[161] In this context, M. Tushnet speaks of absence of a common denominator of values. *Cf.* M. Tushnet, "An essay on rights...," p. 1372.

[162] A. Barak, *Proportionality...*, p. 484.

[163] T.A. Aleinikoff, "Constitutional law in the age...," p. 973.

being granted to the authority that applies this mechanism as its inherent component does not disqualify its rational character.[164]

4.5.5. The Principle of Respecting Constitutional Rights and Freedoms as a Natural Method of Resolving Collisions of Constitutional Rights

Besides the above-described method of resolving collision of constitutional rights by the state at the level of their axiological foundation, the Polish constitutional legislator also points to the existence of a natural method of respecting these rights by the persons concerned. Certainly, if both the parties mutually respect their rights and freedoms, they will naturally restrain themselves in the exercise of their own rights and freedoms in such a way, so that the rights and freedoms of other persons can also be exercised. This particular method of solving constitutional rights' collision found its expression in the content of Art. 31 para. 2 first sentence of the Constitution of the Republic of Poland. According to its wording, 'Everyone shall respect the freedoms and rights of others.' In my view, this obligation is targeted not at state authorities, but private entities being the beneficiaries of constitutional rights and freedoms. Although the constitutional legislator used the term 'everyone' to denote the beholden in this provision, extension of this notion to include state authorities would be contrary to the final part of this provision, where reference is made to freedoms and rights of 'others' (one should add: 'other people who are the holders of these freedoms and rights'). 'Everyone' should therefore be generically similar to the said 'others' and just like them, 'everyone' should be the holder of constitutional rights and freedoms. Reading the content of Art. 31 para. 2 first sentence of the Polish Constitution in this way, we reach a conclusion that anyone who is the subject of constitutional rights and freedoms should respect the rights and freedoms of others who, like him, are the subjects of these rights and freedoms. This would mean that public authorities that are not able to be the beneficiaries of constitutional rights and freedoms cannot be the addressees of this provision. It does not mean that public authorities have no obligation to respect constitutional rights and freedoms, as the one described above. Such obligation arises clearly under Article 30 of the Polish Constitution, according to which respect for dignity of a person, being the source of his rights and freedoms, is the duty of public authorities. Safeguarding rights and freedoms to a man and citizen is also one

---

[164] A. Barak, *Proportionality...*, p. 485. Likewise M. Novak, "Three models of balancing...," p. 103–104.

of the duties of the Republic of Poland, as specified in Article 5 of the Polish Constitution.

Respect for rights and freedoms of other persons referred to in Art. 31 para. 2 of the Polish Constitution can therefore be considered a natural method of solving collisions of constitutional rights. This method does, however, have its limits beyond which the need for state interference in the relations between private entities is justified. Firstly, its effect is conditional upon the balance between the parties to these relations, i.e., the duty to observe constitutional rights being respected by each of them. Absence of such balance as a rule leads to subordination of one party to the other, creating room for compelling a party to do what the law does not prescribe (Art. 31 para. 2, second sentence, of the Polish Constitution). Secondly, applying the natural method of resolving a collision of constitutional rights is possible only in relation to those rights the exercise of which need not be made more precise by the legislator. In practice, this predominantly concerns freedoms, where the legislator's task is to distinguish between them rather than set the conditions for their exercise. If the requirement of a balance between the parties is met, then setting the limits of freedoms by the legislator is secondary in relation to the findings made in this respect by the parties. However, should one of the parties consider that these arrangements violate the obligation of the other party to respect its rights, then reference to the protection by the state will in practice mean recourse to the manner of delimitating the freedoms of both the entities by the state.

Thus, although the natural method of solving the collision of constitutional rights by the concerned parties themselves through a mechanism of mutual respect for rights and freedoms is preferable, as evidenced by it being mentioned in the first place, yet – being aware that the human nature is far from being perfect – the legislator introduces later in the same provision a top-down method of resolving this collision by the state in case the mechanism of mutual respect for rights and freedoms proved insufficient. In this sense, Art. 31 para. 3 of the Polish Constitution establishes a mechanism which is subsidiary to the above-described natural mechanism of resolving a collision of constitutional rights. It is worth noting the dual function of this provision. On the one hand, it grants powers to the legislator to resolve collision of constitutional rights by restricting one right for the sake of protecting the other. This provision clearly states that 'Any limitation upon the exercise of constitutional freedoms and rights may be imposed (…) when necessary (…) for the protection of (…) the freedoms and rights of other persons.' On the other hand, Art. 31 para. 3 of the Constitution of the Republic of Poland is a provision that limits the legislator's interference in relations between private entities, in which a collision of constitutional rights could occur. Indeed, this provision specifies five conditions by which the legislator is bound while defining the principles of resolving this type of collision. Thus, the legislator cannot violate the substance of the colliding rights and freedoms and must ensure their implementation to an appropriate (proportional) degree. As regards the latter condition, its two elements are of particular importance in the process of resolving the collision of constitutional rights, namely the requirement of necessity, also known as non-excessive state interference, and the requirement to balance the values underlying the colliding constitutional rights. These two conditions are mutually correlated. Excessive interference with the rights of an individual is most often the outcome of improper balancing of values underlying the constitutional rights in collision.

4.6. Closing Remarks

In horizontal relations, a collision of constitutional rights is an inevitable phenomenon. It arises from the specific nature of these relations, where both parties are the beneficiaries of rights guaranteed by the constitution. It is, therefore, natural that each party strives for the fullest possible protection of its rights, which creates the need for delineating the sphere of exercise of these rights. Resolving a collision of constitutional rights takes place according to a single universal mechanism, that is, by way of balancing the values underlying these rights. Although this means entanglement of axiology into disputes between private entities, yet there seems to be no alternative for this particular mechanism. The guarantee of fair decisions on collisions of constitutional rights lies in the concept of an objective order of values, according to which constitutional values assume the shape of objective principles that determine the actions of both the legislator and courts. The concept of objective order of values requires of axiological arguments not to be suspended in a vacuum, but be formulated in reference to the text of the constitution.[165] This connection between the reasoning and the legal text expressed in the search for relationships between individual values in the way they are expressed in the Constitution gives an objective dimension to the resolution of collisions between constitutional rights. The relationship of precedence of constitutional rights is first determined in an abstract way by the legislator,

---

[165] S. Jarosz-Żukowska, „Problem horyzontalnego stosowania norm konstytucyjnych...,"
p. 200.

and then collisions between constitutional rights are resolved by courts based on the set legislative framework and again by reference to the constitutional axiology. The mechanism of resolving a collision of constitutional rights is a necessary component of every model of their horizontal application. However, as shown above, the balancing of values within the frame of individual models reveals certain differences.

Chapter 5

ADAPTATIONS OF MODELS OF THE HORIZONTAL EFFECT OF CONSTITUTIONAL RIGHTS AND FREEDOMS IN THE POLISH CONSTITUTIONAL REALITY

In case law there are a few models of the horizontal effect of constitutional rights of an individual, which models are not mutually exclusive, but rather complementary, because to a certain extent they can be applied at the same time. These models can be condensed down to four major ones, i.e. the model of the direct effect of constitutional rights, the model of their indirect effect, the model of the state's protection obligations in horizontal relations and the model of constitutional rights' effect in horizontal relations under the banner of state action. All these models emerged and evolved through judicature, while the role of jurisprudence was mainly to describe them, systematize, justify and provide theoretical support for them. In effect, as a product of courts' activity, these models have not been fossilized and cemented, but can be said to be constantly evolving and developing, taking into account all new changes which occur in the contemporary world.

In my further reflections I attempt to determine the extent to which these models can be implemented in the Polish constitutional reality. However, in these reflections I omit the last of the aforementioned models, i.e. the state action model applied in the US. This model assumes that the Constitution applies in vertical relations only and if it formulates any prohibitions, they are targeted at the state and not an individual. In this model, the notion of 'state action' is understood broadly and covers, subject to certain conditions, also the cases when constitutional rights are actually infringed by a private entity. The US Supreme Court assumes that state actions which violate constitutional rights may include both actions of a private entity discharging, for instance, a public function transferred to it by the state and actions of a private entity supported by the state to such an extent that it is reasonable to attribute the infringements of constitutional rights perpetrated by that entity directly to the state. But the basic assumption of the model, namely that the Constitution applies in vertical relations only, is not approved in the Polish jurisprudence and judicature, and even though some of its solutions can apply to the Polish constitutional reality, I decided to leave it out of the further reflections due to its particularities.

5.1. The Model of the Direct Horizontal Effect of Constitutional Rights

5.1.1. Preliminary Remarks

We speak of the direct horizontal effect of constitutional rights when a private entity can invoke them directly in the relations with another private entity, which, in this configuration, is at the same time the beholden entity. The former may pursue protection of its rights and freedoms and defend itself against the claims of another private entity solely on the basis of the constitutional provisions and indicating them as the source of obligations borne by the latter entity. An infringement of constitutional rights or freedoms by the beholden entity entails adverse consequences for the latter. The direct horizontal effect of constitutional rights has a subsidiary character, thus it can only come into play when constitutional rights are not sufficiently protected at the statutory level.[166] It is only then that it becomes necessary to directly invoke a provision of the fundamental law in relations with another private entity.

If one is to benefit from the direct effect of constitutional rights, a few preliminary conditions have to be met. Firstly, the constitutional provisions establishing the rights and freedoms which might potentially operate in horizontal relations must be capable of autonomous application, so that they can be the sole grounds for claims resulting from infringement of these rights or freedoms. Secondly, private entities must by the addressees of such rights and freedoms, not only as the beneficiaries, but also as the beholden. Thirdly, the constitutional provisions must provide for specific obligations on the part of private entities, such obligations correlated with the rights and freedoms of other private entities. Fourthly, there must exist sanctions for infringements of constitutional rights and freedoms which might be triggered if a private entity's claim alleging infringement of its constitutional rights and freedoms by another private entity is granted.

---

[166] *Cf.* Z. Kędzia, *Burżuazyjna koncepcja praw człowieka*, Wrocław–Warszawa–Kraków–Gdańsk 1980, p. 285; W. Osiatyński, *Prawa człowieka i ich granice*, Kraków 2011, p. 306–307; B. Skwara, "Horyzontalne obowiązywanie...," p. 173.

5.1.2. Characteristics of the Model Based on Examples of States Where it is Applied

The conception of the direct horizontal effect of constitutional rights is applied e.g. in Germany (albeit to a very limited extent)[167] and in Ireland.[168] But it should be emphasized that the constitutions of both these states do not expressly refer to the problem of the horizontal effect of the individual's rights that they regulate. In both cases, the validity of the conception was justified by references to general provisions which oblige the state, not other individuals, to respect the rights of an individual. In the German Constitution this was Art. 1 para. 3, while in the Irish Constitution – Art. 40 para. 3. The first of these provisions states that 'The following basic rights shall bind the legislature, the executive and the judiciary as directly applicable law.' In turn, pursuant to Art. 40 para. 3 of the Constitution of Ireland, 'The State guarantees in its laws to respect, and, as far as practicable, by its laws to defend and vindicate the personal rights of the citizen' (subpara. 1) and 'The State shall, in particular, by its laws protect as best it may from unjust attack and, in the case of injustice done, vindicate the life, person, good name, and property rights of every citizen' (subpara. 2). Thus, what follows from both provisions is that it is the state that is bound by constitutional rights. Art. 1 para. 3 of the German Constitution stresses the duty of public authorities to respect these rights, while Art. 40 para. 3 of the Constitution of Ireland emphasizes the duty to protect them.

Characteristically, in both states the above provisions are ascribed a much broader meaning than what results from their literal interpretation. In the German literature it is stressed that Art. 1 para. 3 of the German Constitution does not include an exhaustive list of entities which are bound by fundamental rights, but only indicates the manner in which entities holding power are bound by these rights.[169] The intention of this provision is to stress that fundamental rights have a normative character and, as 'directly applicable law,'

---

[167] Cf. W. Reimers, *Die Bedeutung der Grundrechte für das Privatrecht*, 1958, p. 20; G. Vogt, *Die Drittwirkung der Grundrechte und Grundrechtsbestimmungen des Bonner Grundgesetzes*, Münster 1960, p. 226.

[168] A.S. Butler, "Constitutional rights in private litigation: a Critique and comparative analysis," *Anglo-American Law Review*, 22 (1993), p. 20; C. O'Cinneide, "Irish constitutional law and direct horizontal effect – a successful experiment?" (in:) D. Oliver, J. Fedtke (eds.), *Human Rights and the Private Sphere. A Comparative Study*, New York 2007; M. Hunt, "The 'Horizontal Effect' of the Human Rights Act," *Public Law*, 1998, p. 428–429; A. Clapham, *Human Rights Obligations of Non-State Actors*, New York 2006, p. 441.

[169] C.W. Canaris, *Grundrechte und Privatrechte*, Berlin–New York 1999, p. 15–16; H. Linders, *Über der Frage der unmittelbaren Beteutung der Grundrechtsbestimmungen des Bonner*

they bind state authorities. This interpretation leads to the conclusion that Art. 1 para. 3 of the German Constitution at least does not exclude the horizontal effect of fundamental rights. In turn in Ireland it is assumed that Art. 40 para. 3 of the Constitution gives every citizen the right to sue in court not only the state, when such a state fails to discharge the obligation of providing the necessary protection by adopting the relevant statutes, but also another citizen who infringes the constitutional rights of the person concerned.[170] In other words, what is inferred from the state's duty to protect the rights of an individual enshrined in this provision is the duty of respect for such rights on the part of private entities against whose activities the state should protect the individual.

Both in Germany and in Ireland constitutional rights are treated not only as subjective rights, but also as objective principles which bind state authorities, in particular courts resolving disputes between private entities.[171] In Germany it is stressed that certain fundamental rights enshrined in the Constitution are not only freedom-related rights addressed against the state, but mainly principles of order in community life, which are of direct importance for legal relations between citizens. Agreements, unilateral acts in law and other measures taken by private entities cannot contradict these principles.[172] Meanwhile, in Ireland it is stressed that the court needs to interpret private law norms taking into account constitutional rights when these norms do not guarantee sufficient protection.[173]

An additional argument which should speak in favor of the direct horizontal effect of some constitutional rights is the contents of provisions which enshrine these rights. It is pointed out that these provisions are addressed to private entities, that they impose duties on such entities and that sometimes they even introduce sanctions for their infringements. In Germany, direct horizontal dimension is currently incontestably ascribed to Art. 9 para. 3, second sentence, of the Constitution, which provides that agreements re-

---

Grundgesetzes für der privatrechtlichen Rechtsverkehr (Ein Beitrag zum Problem der „Drittwirkung" der Grundrechtsbestimmungen), Münster 1961, p. 63–64.

[170] J. Temple Lang, "Private law aspects of the irish constitution," *Irish Jurist* 6 (1971), p. 246–247.

[171] C. O'Cinneide, "Irish constitutional law....," p. 216–217.

[172] H.C. Nipperdey, "Gleicher Lohn der Frau für gleiche Leistung. Ein Beitrag zur Auslegung der Grundrechte," *Recht der Arbeit*, 1950, p. 121 et. seq.; A. Guckelberger, "Die Drittwirkung der Grundrechte...," p. 1153; P. Egli, *Drittwirkung von Grundrechten. Zugleich ein Beitrag zur Dogmatik der grundrechtlichen Schutzpflichten im Schweizer Recht*, Zurich 2002, p. 18; T. Langer, *Die Problematik der Geltung...*, p. 56.

[173] J. Temple Lang, "Private law aspects...," p. 254; M. Forde, *Constitutional Law*, Dublin 2004, p. 833–834.

straining the right to form associations to safeguard and improve working and economic conditions or impairing the enjoyment of the said right are null and void, while measures directed to this end are unlawful. In addition, some German legal scholars attribute direct horizontal effect also to rights regulated in Art. 20 para. 4 of the German Constitution (right to resist any person seeking to abolish constitutional order) and Art. 48 of the German Constitution (employee's rights relating to standing for election to the Bundestag and exercising the office), as well as Art. 1 para. 1, first sentence, of the German Constitution (human dignity) and Art. 3 para. 3 of the German Constitution (prohibition of discrimination). In Ireland direct horizontal effect is attributed mainly to the freedom of association in trade unions, referred to in Art. 40 para. 6 subpara. 1 item iii of the Constitution of that state.

Both in Germany and in Ireland, the development of doctrine of direct horizontal effect of constitutional rights took place in the period after World War II. In Germany the doctrine was first applied by the Federal Labor Court *(Bundearbeitsgericht)* and the Federal Court of Justice *(Bundesgerichtshof)* in mid-1950s, while in Ireland by the Supreme Court in early 1960s. In the latter state it was not until the first half of the 1970s that the conception of constitutional tort was formulated. Both in Germany and in Ireland it was labor-related case law that had fundamental importance for the development of this doctrine.[174] The Federal Labor Court assessed from the fundamental rights' perspective certain actions of employers, such as termination of an employment contract due to the employee's fault (in the context of freedom of speech),[175] or including a celibacy clause in the employment contract (in the context of human dignity and protection of family).[176] The Irish Supreme Court most often considered the problem in cases in which objections of infringement of the freedom of membership in a trade union and the freedom to remain outside its structures were raised, regardless of whether employee rights were infringed by the employer or by trade unions.[177] Apart from

---

[174] P. Egli, *Drittwirkung von Grundrechten...*, p. 20; U. Preuß, „The German Drittwirkung doctrine and its socio-political background" (in:) A. Sajo, R. Uitz (eds.), *The Constitution in Private Relations: Expanding Constitutionalism*, Utrecht 2005, p. 24. Similarly cf. M. Avbelj, "Is there Drittwirkung in EU law?" (in:) A. Sajo, R. Uitz (eds.), *The Constitution in Private Relation: Expanding Constitutionalism*, Utrecht 2005, p. 154.

[175] Judgment of the Federal Labor Court of December 3, 1954, Ref. No. 1 AZR 150/54, BAGE 1, 185 (*Kündigung eines Betriebsratsmitglieds*).

[176] Judgment of the Federal Labor Court of May 10, 1957, Ref. No. 1 AZR 249/57, BAGE 4, 274 (*Zölibatsklausel*).

[177] Judgments of the Irish Supreme Court in cases: *Educational Company of Ireland Ltd v. Fitzpatrick*, (1961) I.R. 345; *East Donegal Co-Operative Livestock Mart v. A.-G.* (1970) IR 317; *Meskell v. Coras Iompair Eireann*, (1973) I.R.121; *Glover v BLN Ltd*, (1973) I.R. 388.

labor law cases, the doctrine of direct horizontal effect was developed in both countries in cases concerning protection of personal interests and contractual relations.

In the 1980s in Germany we can see a retreat from the conception of the direct horizontal effect of fundamental rights in favor of the conception of their indirect effect, while in Ireland the former conception grew weaker and the latter was adopted to a narrow extent. In Germany the trend is illustrated by cases indicating the need for a private employer to respect an employee's fundamental rights in the process of concretizing the labor relation.[178] In such concretization, the employer should taking into account equitable principles (*billige Ermessen*), whose substance is determined by the fundamental rights. Therefore, those judgements stressed the importance of the general clause contained in a statutory provision. Yet due to the fact that the duty to interpret provisions taking into account fundamental rights was placed upon the employer, these judgments are quoted in German literature as examples of judgements implementing the conception of the direct horizontal effect of fundamental rights. Nevertheless in the 1980s the Federal Labor Court issued the first judgments in which it expressly accepted the conception already applied in case law of the Federal Constitutional Court, that is, the conception of the indirect horizontal effect of fundamental rights. It is worthwhile to remind, for instance, a 1986 judgment on the lawfulness of the employer's gathering and processing of data concerning employees' work-related telephone conversations.[179] In that judgment the Federal Labor Court found that the confidentiality of communications did not apply directly in horizontal relations, but was an important constitutional value, which needed to be taken into account in these relations as one of the so-called basic tenets of the Constitution of the Federal Republic of Germany. These tenets are an element of the objective order of values resulting from the constitutional chapter on fundamental rights and apply across all branches of law, including private law.

Also in Ireland, the 1980s saw a weakening of the conception of the direct horizontal effect of constitutional rights. The Supreme Court started to emphasize the subsidiary nature of constitutional tort formulated on the basis of constitutional provisions with respect to claims for protection of consti-

---

[178] Judgments of the Federal Labor Court: of December 20, 1984, Ref. No. 2 AZR 436/82, NJW nr 85/1986; of May 24, 1989, Ref. No. 2 AZR 285/88, BAGE 62, 59 (*Medikamententwicklung für Nuklearkrieg*).

[179] Judgment of the Federal Labor Court of May 27, 1986, Ref. No. 1 ABR 48/84, BAGE 52, 88 (*Telefongespräche*).

tutional rights, grounded in enactments or common law.[180] The belief that the constitutional protection of rights of an individual was subsidiary vis--à-vis the protection guaranteed by other binding normative acts (in Ireland also by precedents) can nowadays be seen as a typical element of the model of the direct horizontal effect of individual's rights. The Irish conception of constitutional tort assumes that it is only if there are no other possibilities of protecting an individual's constitutional right that such protection should be derived from the constitutional provision which enshrines the said right. Similarly, the German Federal Court of Justice granted private entities the possibility to invoke in horizontal relations the so-called general right of personality (*allgemeine Persönlichkeitsrecht*), resulting from Art. 1 and Art. 2 of the German Constitution, when the given right was not protected by statutory provisions.[181] The Federal Labor Court also derived protection of the employee's fundamental rights from statutory provisions in the first place and only if there were none, like in the case Art. 9 para. 3, second sentence, of the German Constitution, did it derive such protection directly from a constitutional provision.

Nowadays in Germany direct horizontal effect is unquestionably ascribed only to Art. 9 para. 3, second sentence, of the German Constitution. The conception which is of vital importance in this regard is the indirect horizontal effect of fundamental rights; in comparison, the conception of direct horizontal effect is of marginal importance. In Ireland it is accepted that the conception of indirect horizontal effect should supplement the traditional conception of direct horizontal effect. Only if it is found that existing legal norms do not adequately protect constitutional rights, should courts apply constitutional rights in the process of interpreting and developing norms of the private law. As assumed by the Irish Supreme Court and legal academics, the state's failure to implement constitutional safeguards is an argument justifying the court invoking the doctrine of direct horizontal effect of constitutional rights. If the state protects constitutional rights in a completely inadequate manner, this constitutes the grounds for court intervention taking the form of giving that right indirect horizontal effect.

---

[180] Judgments of the Irish Supreme Court in cases: *Hanrahan v. Merck Sharp and Dohme*, (1988) I.R. 629; *McDonnell v Ireland*, (1998) 1 I.R. 134.

[181] Judgments of the German Federal Court of Justice: of May 25, 1954, Ref. No. I ZR 211/53, NJW 1954, p. 1404–1405; of February 14, 1958, Ref. No. I ZR 151/56, BGHZ 26, 349 (*Herrenreiter*); of March 18, 1959, Ref. No. IV ZR 182/58, NJW 1959, p. 1269–1271; of April 26, 1972, Ref. No. IV ZR 18/71, NJW 1972, p. 1414–1415; of April 28, 1986, Ref. No. II ZR 254/85, NJW 1986, p. 2944–2945.

5.1.3. Rights and Freedoms in the Polish Constitution which are Capable of Direct Horizontal Effect

Among the constitutional rights and freedoms we can distinguish those which apply only in vertical relations and those which can also apply in horizontal relations. The former make an individual the right holder and the state the beholden, while the latter put also other individuals along with the state on the side of the beholden. An example of a constitutional right which has the vertical dimension only is the right of access to public services, while examples of rights or freedoms which may also have the horizontal dimension include the right to strike and the freedom of speech. Yet it is not easy to isolate the category of rights having exclusively the vertical dimension. As an example we can mention the right of access to court, which seems to be a classic right belonging to this category, but can be infringed by a private entity which purposefully prolongs court proceedings and thus prevents another private entity from exercising the right guaranteed by Art. 45 para. 1 of the Constitution to have a case heard without undue delay.

The problem of the direct horizontal effect of constitutional rights can be considered only with regard to those rights that are capable of application in relations between private entities. In addition, rights of this kind have to be established by constitutional provisions which may be applied autonomously and, therefore, in case of a dispute between private entities, may constitute autonomous grounds for court decisions. The autonomous application of constitutional provisions, as has already been said, requires that two conditions be met. Firstly, a constitutional provision which establishes a certain right or freedom must be formulated sufficiently precisely and unequivocally that an individual case can be resolved solely on its grounds. Secondly, the matter regulated in that provision cannot be the subject of a binding statutory regulation, because autonomous application of a constitutional right cannot lead to bypassing it.

The direct horizontal effect of constitutional rights undoubtedly has an exceptional nature. Firstly, because most constitutional provisions which establish rights or freedoms are further elaborated in statutory regulations which, in case of a dispute between private entities, become the legal grounds for court decisions. Secondly, not all constitutional provisions which establish rights or freedoms having the horizontal dimension are precise enough to enable an individual case to be resolved on their basis alone.[182] This does

---

[182] Similarly *cf.* P. Lindenbergh, "Fundamental rights in private law. Anchors or goals in a globalizing legal order?" (in:) M. Faure, A. van der Walt (eds.), *Globalization and Private Law. The Way Forward*, Cheltenham 2010, p. 380.

not mean, however, that in the context of the Polish Constitution it is impossible to adopt and apply the conception of the direct horizontal effect of constitutional rights. There exist rights that have not been 'wrapped' in a statutory regulation, such as the right to submit petitions, which can be addressed, among others, to 'organizations and social institutions in connection with the performance of their prescribed duties within the field of public administration' (Art. 63 of the Constitution).[183] In turn, in case of constitutional rights that did become the subject of statutory regulation, the need for their direct horizontal application may arise when the existing statutory regulation is perceived to be incomplete or is found unconstitutional by the Constitutional Tribunal, upon which it loses its binding force. And if the first condition for the autonomous application of constitutional provisions, namely lack of statutory regulation, is met, then we should only consider which specific constitutional rights and freedoms are precise enough to be capable of direct application. Their precise character has to be determined from the point of view of the three conditions for the horizontal effect of constitutional rights, i.e. the beholden entity, the substance of the obligation and the sanction for its infringement.

In order to demonstrate the functionality of that conception, it is worthwhile to mention the prohibition of using corporal punishment on children, which until August 1, 2010, was not included in ordinary legislation.[184] Meanwhile Art. 40 of the Constitution, which reads 'application of corporal punishment shall be prohibited' was in force then and still remains in force. Although the place of this provision, before Art. 41 to Art. 44 of the Constitution, might suggest that it concerns criminal procedure and thus establishes a prohibition the state using corporal punishment, but there is no such express limitation in Art. 40 of the Constitution. This would lead to the conclusion that the prohibition of corporal punishment applied from the moment the Constitution entered into force in both vertical and horizontal relations,[185] so also children could invoke this prohibition in relations with

---

[183] Cf. M. Florczak-Wątor, "O potrzebie ustawowego uregulowania trybu rozpatrywania petycji" (in:) Zeszyty Prawnicze BAS, 2 (2013), p. 25 et. seq. The first Act on Petitions was adopted in Poland as late as on July 11, 2014 (Official Journal of Laws (Dz. U.), item 1195) and will enter into force on 6 September 2015.

[184] Naturally, apart from the most drastic cases of violating the prohibition, penalized in criminal law, such as battery or child abuse.

[185] This opinion is supported by L. Bosek, who states: 'It would be difficult to say, for example, that the prohibition of torture is not addressed to private entitiep.' Cf. idem, Gwarancje godności ludzkiej i ich wpływ na polskie prawo cywilne, Warszawa 2012, p. 123. Similarly cf. A. Wyrozumska, "Direct application of the Polish constitution and international treaties to private conduct," Polish Yearbook of International Law, 25 (2001), p. 8.

parents. Given such an interpretation of Art. 40 of the Constitution, a conclusion should be drawn that Art. 96¹, added to the [Polish] Family and Guardianship Code [FGC] on August 1, 2010, did not introduce a prohibition of the use of corporal punishment by those who had parental authority or custody, or took care of minors, but repeated in this scope the prohibition which had earlier been introduced by Art. 40 of the Constitution. But if we assumed a different interpretation and held that the latter provision applied in vertical relations only, then Art. 96¹ FGC would have a constitutive character, establishing a similar prohibition in horizontal relations, more specifically, in the relations between parents and children. What follows from the governmental bill amending the Act on Counteracting Domestic Violence and Certain Other Statutes[186] is that the promoters of Art. 96¹ FGC were rather of the latter opinion. However, the opposite standpoint on the issue, according to which the ban on use of corporal punishment results expressly from Art. 40 of the Polish Constitution, was presented in experts' opinions prepared for the purposes of the legislative procedure.[187]

In my view, Art. 40 of the Constitution is indeed an example of a provision which could and should have been applied directly in horizontal relations, including those between parents and children.[188] Before August 1, 2010 there already existed conditions for the autonomous application of this provision, because the resulting prohibition of corporal punishment is clear and precise and prior to that date it had not been regulated separately in statutory law. Currently, we should read similarly Art. 39 of the Constitution. It contains a prohibition of subjecting citizens to scientific experimentation, including medical experimentation, without their voluntary consent, which prohibition is addressed not only to state-owned, but also private research institutes. Hence it is a provision which can apply directly in horizontal relations.

---

[186] Sejm paper No. 1698.

[187] *Cf.* legal opinions by A. Sakowicz, dated January 27, 2010, and E. Zielińska, dated March 15, 2010, available on website http://orka.sejm.gov.pl/rexdomk6.nsf/Opdodr?OpenPage&-No.=1698 (accessed on June 23, 2015).

[188] Other provisions which might be applied in the same way are – also relating to the parent-child relationships – Art. 48 para. 1, second sentence, and Art. 53 para. 3 of the Constitution. On this subject *cf.* S. Jarosz-Żukowska, "Problem horyzontalnego stosowania...," p. 201–202.

5.1.4. Private Entities as Entities Beholden to Implement Constitutional Rights and Freedoms

The conception of the direct horizontal effect of constitutional rights assumes that private entities are not only beneficiaries of constitutional rights and freedoms, that is, right holders, but also entities beholden by rights and freedoms of other entities and this subsection is devoted precisely to this issue. In this context we should explain that we can speak of an obligation borne by a given entity when a certain behavior of that entity is required or prohibited by the binding legal norm.[189]

There are no doubts that public authorities always have obligations concerning the satisfaction of constitutional rights and freedoms of an individual. These authorities are the only beholden in the case of constitutional rights which operate in vertical relations. Even when constitutional provisions do not expressly formulate the obligation to implement such rights, there are no doubts that it is an obligation of public authorities. In order to illustrate this thesis it is worthwhile to refer to Art. 55 para. 1 of the Constitution, pursuant to which 'The extradition of a Polish citizen shall be prohibited (...)'. This provision does not identify the addressee of the prohibition it expresses, nevertheless, due to the fact that the extradition decision is taken and enforced by public authorities, it is beyond doubt that this prohibition is addressed precisely to these authorities. Art. 31 para. 1 of the Constitution, pursuant to which 'Freedom of the person shall receive legal protection,' can be interpreted in a similar way. Since legal protection can only be guaranteed by the state, the obligation to establish it rests with public authorities.

Most constitutional rights and freedoms can, however, operate also in horizontal relations, which begs the question whether, in the light of the Constitution, a private entity can be beholden by such rights and freedoms. As constitutional provisions hardly ever mention private entities as those obliged to implement rights and freedoms, this conclusion can only be formulated on the basis of results of systemic and functional interpretation.[190]

Firstly, the problem concerns cases when the obligation to take specific measures which serve to implement constitutional rights and freedoms is formulated in an impersonal manner, without naming the beholden, and

---

[189] Cf. Z. Ziembiński, "O normie prawnej" (in:) P. Wronkowska (ed.), *Z teorii i filozofii prawa Zygmunta Ziembińskiego*, Łódź 2007, p. 34; P. Wronkowska (in:) P. Wronkowska, Z. Ziembiński, *Zarys teorii prawa*, Poznań 2001, p. 101.

[190] K. Wojtyczek, "Horyzontalny wymiar praw człowieka zagwarantowanych w Konstytucji RP," *Kwartalnik Prawa Prywatnego*, 2 (1999), p. 229.

public authorities do not have a monopoly in discharging this obligation. These are mainly provisions formulating the obligation to ensure a specific freedom. Some of them use the formula '(…) shall be ensured to everyone,' for instance 'freedom of conscience and religion' (Art. 53 para. 1), 'freedom to express opinions, to acquire and to disseminate information' (Art. 54 para. 1), 'freedom of peaceful assembly and participation in such assemblies' (Art. 57), 'freedom of association' (Art. 58). In other provisions, the expression is '(…) shall be ensured,' without naming the right holder, e.g. 'freedom and privacy of communication' (Art. 49), 'inviolability of the home' (Art. 50), 'freedom of association in trade unions' (Art. 59 para. 1). The obligation to ensure the freedom is borne by a different entity than the one enjoying that freedom. Thus the beholden may be the state if we understand 'ensuring' a certain right as tantamount to 'guaranteeing' it; likewise, a private entity may be one if 'ensuring' a right is understood as just 'respecting' it.

Secondly, some provisions of the Constitution not only fail to name the beholden, but even contain no express indication of the duties correlated with the right or freedom formulated in these provisions. These provisions are, as it were, the reverse of the provisions containing program norms. While in the latter case there are no doubts that they establish certain obligations, and the doubts concern the possibility of deducing any subjective rights from them, the provisions in the group in question do not give rise to doubts as to the possibility of inferring specific rights, but as to whether specific obligations can be formulated on their basis. This concerns provisions which use the formula in which specific entities 'shall have the right to' do certain things. Examples from this group of provisions include Art. 35 para. 2 ('National and ethnic minorities shall have the right to establish educational and cultural institutions, institutions designed to protect religious identity, as well as to participate in the resolution of matters connected with their cultural identity') or Art. 47 ('Everyone shall have the right to legal protection of his private and family life, of his honor and good reputation and to make decisions about his personal life'). In the case of economic, social and cultural rights and freedoms, the formula 'a citizen shall have the right to (…)' is usually accompanied by the state's obligation to issue a statute concretizing that right (e.g. Art. 66 para. 1, Art. 67, Art. 68, Art. 70 para. 1). From provisions of this kind one can only infer private entities' obligation to respect the rights established by these provisions, which means, like in the first group of provisions mentioned above, only negative obligations.

Thirdly, some constitutional provisions formulate imperatives or prohibitions without naming the beholden, which leads to the conclusion that not only public authorities, but also private entities, can be their addressees. In this group of provisions we should mention, first of all, Art. 31 para. 2 ('No one shall be compelled to do that which is not required by law') and Art. 32 para. 2 ('No one shall be discriminated against in political, social or economic life for any reason whatsoever'). Unlike addressees of the principle of equality from Art. 32 para. 1 of the Constitution, the addressees of the prohibition of discrimination, which both the quoted provisions refer to, are not clearly identified, which may mean that the constitutional legislator wanted to extend the effect of these prohibitions to include private relations.[191]

Other examples of provisions that do not clarify the addressees of the prohibitions they introduce include Art. 51 para. 1 ('No one may be obliged, except on the basis of statute, to disclose information concerning his person') and Art. 53 para. 6 ('No one shall be compelled to participate or not participate in religious practices'). Yet another provision from this group is Art. 30 of the Constitution, pursuant to which human dignity is inviolable. The resulting prohibition of violating human dignity has, like the above prohibitions, a universal character, which means that not only public authorities are its addressees, but private entities too.[192]

Fourthly, some constitutional provisions grant an individual certain rights which the individual can only exercise in horizontal relations, that is, relations with other individuals. At the same time, these provisions do not expressly name the entity that should respect such rights. Moreover, in their contents one can hardly find any obligations that might apply to public authorities. As an example, we can mention the provisions concerning parents' rights vis-à-vis their children, i.e. the right to bring up children in accordance with the parents' convictions (Art. 48 para. 1, first sentence, of the Constitution) and the right to ensure that children receive a moral and religious upbringing and teaching in accordance with the parents' convictions (Art. 53 para. 3 of the Constitution). Pursuant to the second sentence of Art. 48 para. 1, which applies accordingly also to the right regulated in Art. 53 para. 3 of the Constitution, 'Such upbringing shall respect the degree of maturity of a child as well as his freedom of conscience and belief and also his convictions.' This

---

[191] M. Masternak-Kubiak, "Prawo do równego traktowania" (in:) B. Banaszak, A. Preisner (eds.), *Prawa i wolności obywatelskie w Konstytucji RP*, Warszawa 2002, p. 136. Similarly *cf.* K. Wojtyczek, "Horyzontalny wymiar praw…," p. 243; A. Wyrozumska, "Direct application of the Polish…," p. 8; M. Safjan, „Efekt horyzontalny…," p. 316; S. Jarosz-Żukowska, "Problem horyzontalnego stosowania…," p. 207–208.

[192] B. Banaszak, "Prawa człowieka i obywatela…," p. 57; M. Safjan, "Refleksje wokół konstytucyjnych uwarunkowań rozwoju ochrony dóbr osobistych," *Kwartalnik Prawa Prywatnego*, 1 (2002), p. 227; P. Tuleja, "Stosowanie Konstytucji RP…," p. 125; B. Skwara, "Poziome obowiązywanie praw człowieka w świetle Konstytucji RP," *Homines Hominibus*, 1 (2009), p. 52; L. Bosek, *Gwarancje godności ludzkiej…*, p. 121.

provision should be read as one obliging parents who bring up children to consider the degree of maturity of the latter, as well as their freedom of conscience and belief, and convictions. When we interpret it this way, parents are not only the holders of the right to rear children in accordance with their own convictions, but also the beholden to ensure certain rights and freedoms that their children are guaranteed, i.e. freedom of conscience and religion, freedom of convictions, as well as the right to decide about themselves to the extent resulting from the degree of maturity they reached.

Likewise, in horizontal relations, and more specifically in relations between trade unions and employers and their organizations, there apply the rights regulated in Art. 59 para. 2, i.e. the right to bargain, particularly for the purpose of resolving collective disputes, and to conclude collective labor agreements and other arrangements. In this case, the holders of both rights are trade unions and employers or their organizations, thus a question arises who is beholden by these rights, in other words, who might infringe these rights. Once the right is effective only between two private entities, then the right of one of them is accompanied by the other entity's obligation to respect it. This way, we reach the conclusion that both trade unions and employers (employer organization) can be the beholden under Art. 59 para. 2 of the Constitution. A similar direction should be taken in interpreting Art. 59 para. 3 of the Constitution, which gives trade unions the right to organize workers' strikes or other forms of protest subject to limitations specified by statute. In this case, the employer is not named as the entity obliged to respect this right, but considering that it is the addressee of demands voiced by the workers on strike, it obviously must have certain obligations correlated with the right to organize strikes. In the context of employee relations, we should also turn our attention to two subsequent provisions. Pursuant to Art. 65 para. 3 of the Constitution, permanent employment of children under 16 years of age is prohibited. In this case, there arises a question about the addressee of this very specific prohibition. Naturally, once again we should consider that it is addressed to every employer, because it is them that can employ children in contravention of this provision. In turn, Art. 66 of the Constitution guarantees employees the right to safe and hygienic conditions of work and the right to statutorily specified days free from work and annual paid holidays. These, too, are typical rights implemented in horizontal relations, which is why the employer is obliged to respect them. As for the former right, this is expressly indicated in the second sentence of Art. 66 para. 1 of the Constitution, which provides that 'the obligations of employers shall be specified by statute.'

The above reflections lead to the conclusion that, more or less expressly, some constitutional provisions concerning rights and duties make private entities, not necessarily even those functionally connected with the state, the beholden. It should be noted that in two cases only does the Polish Constitution expressly mention the obligations that some private entities have towards other private entities. Pursuant to Art. 31 para. 2 of the Constitution, 'everyone shall respect the freedoms and rights of others,' while pursuant to Art. 72 para. 3 of the Constitution, in the course of establishing the rights of a child, persons responsible for children must consider and, insofar as possible, give priority to the views of the child. While the latter provision has a narrow scope of application, the former is one of the general principles of rights and freedoms of a person and citizen. This is confirmed by its place in a subsection of Chapter II entitled 'General Principles.' According to Krzysztof Wojtyczek, from Art. 31 para. 2, first sentence, of the Constitution 'it follows unequivocally that the constitutional legislator strives to ensure the protection of human rights on the horizontal plane. Controversies may concern only the way in which these rights should be implemented in relations between private entities.'[193] In other words, it is possible to read Art. 31 para. 2, first sentence, of the Constitution from a broader perspective, as the legal grounds for the horizontal effect of all constitutional rights and freedoms, if only they are not limited to vertical relations by their nature. The Polish Constitutional Tribunal seems to assume a similar standpoint. In its judgment dated April 29, 2003, Ref. No. SK 24/02, the Tribunal held: 'the obligation to respect human freedom applies, in accordance with Art. 31 para. 2, first sentence, of the Constitution, not only in relations of a person and citizen with the state and public authorities, but also in relations between individuals themselves. It results to the fullest extent from Art. 31 paras. 1 and 2 of the Constitution that nobody can be forced to enter into a contract or prohibited from entering it, or forced to choose a certain counterparty, or to include specific clauses in the contract, unless the law provides otherwise. This limitation affects everyone to the same extent. Human freedom understood this way, naturally being just a certain "small part" of the whole sphere of human freedom, enjoys constitutional protection.'

We should also bear in mind that one of the obligations of a person and citizen, expressly stated in Art. 83 of the Constitution, is to 'observe the law of the Republic of Poland.' The Constitution is also a component element of that law, as explicitly confirmed in its Art. 8 para. 1: 'The Constitution shall be the supreme law of the Republic of Poland.' So, if quite a lot of constitutional

---

[193] K. Wojtyczek, "Horyzontalny wymiar praw...," p. 229; M. Masternak-Kubiak, "Prawo do równego...," p. 135.

provisions concern the rights and freedoms of an individual, we can say that each private entity has an obligation to respect them. And in this very obligation we can notice the need for some private entities to respect constitutional rights and freedoms of other private entities, i.e. in horizontal relations. Art. 83 of the Constitution enables us to formulate similar general conclusions concerning the horizontal nature of all rights and freedoms as Art. 31 para. 2, first sentence, of the Constitution, which was mentioned earlier.

5.1.5. Obligations Correlated with Constitutional Rights and Freedoms

Another condition for the direct horizontal effect of constitutional rights is establishing that the constitutional provisions concerning rights and duties impose specific obligations on the entity obliged to respect them.

First, however, we should indicate the obligations of public authorities, because to some extent they are linked with the obligations of private entities. The first one is the obligation to refrain from any actions which interfere with the sphere of an individual's freedom. An obligation of this kind may be inferred both from the provisions that prohibit certain behaviors (e.g. Art. 39, Art. 40, Art. 53 paras. 6 and 7 of the Constitution) and from provisions which set forth the conditions for limiting the constitutional rights and freedoms (Art. 31 para. 3 of the Constitution). The second obligation of public authorities is to create conditions for implementing constitutional rights and freedoms. This obligation concerns particularly the situations when the constitutional provisions delegates a matter related to a constitutional right or freedom to be regulated in a statute (e.g. Art. 41 para. 1, Art. 49, Art. 50, Art. 52 para. 3 of the Constitution), which occurs most often in the case of social, economic and cultural freedoms and rights. The third obligation is to protect the rights and freedoms of one entity against interference by other entities, including private ones. An obligation of this kind is expressly worded in Art. 76 of the Constitution, which provides that 'Public authorities shall protect consumers, customers, hirers or lessees against activities threatening their health, privacy and safety, as well as against dishonest market practices.' Other obligations of public authorities include the protection of dignity (Art. 30) or of the rights of the child (Art. 72 para. 1). Legal protection is also accorded to the freedom of the person (Art. 31 para. 1), life (Art. 38), as well as ownership and the right of succession (Art. 64 para. 2). Some constitutional provisions declare protecting a given right or freedom without naming the entity which should ensure such protection, for instance Art. 47 ('Everyone shall have the right to legal protection of his private and family life, of his honor and good reputation and to make decisions about his personal life'), Art. 49 ('The freedom and privacy of communication shall be ensured') and Art. 68 para 1 ('Everyone shall have the right to have his health protected'). Protecting the rights and freedoms of an individual is also a value that justifies the need to limit the enjoyment of constitutional rights and freedoms (Art. 31 para. 3, Art. 53 para. 5, Art. 61 para. 3). The protective obligations borne by the state are yet another argument in favor of the horizontal effect of some constitutional rights and freedoms. It is obvious that the state protects an individual not so much against its own actions, but against actions of non-state entities, that is, private ones. This is clearly stated in Art. 76 of the Constitution, which mentions public authorities protecting consumers, customers, hirers or lessees against for instance 'unfair market practices' resulting from actions of private entities.

By contrast, private entities have mainly negative obligations, expressed by the prohibition of interference with the sphere of a constitutionally protected freedom. Prohibitions of universal character apply to them, including the prohibition of using torture and cruel, inhuman or degrading treatment of other people (Art. 40) or the prohibition of compelling anyone to participate or not participate in religious practices (Art. 53 para. 6). All these prohibitions are connected with freedoms which, by their very nature, are absolute. The view that freedoms of an individual have horizontal effect was expressed by the Constitutional Tribunal in the judgment issued on February 18, 2004, Ref. No. P 21/02, where it held: 'The positive aspect of "freedoms of an individual" means that an individual may freely model his behavior in a given sphere, choosing such forms of activity which suit him the most or refraining from any activity. The negative aspect of "freedoms of an individual" consists in a legal obligation to refrain – or stop anyone else – from interference in the sphere reserved for an individual. This is an obligation for both the state and other entities.'

A negative obligation of private entities results also from Art. 30 of the Constitution, pursuant to which human dignity is inviolable and its protection is a duty of public authorities. Such a formulation leads to the conclusion that dignity may not be violated by public authorities as the addressees of the obligation to respect it, which is specified in this provision, as well as by private entities and it is against the latter's activities that public authorities are obliged to protect human dignity. The universal character of the prohibition of violating human dignity makes sense only when it is addressed to all entities, including private ones.[194] Such a standpoint is also assumed by the Polish Constitutional Tribunal when it states that 'The prohibition of violating human dignity has an

---

[194] *Cf.* B. Banaszak, "Prawa człowieka i obywatela…," p. 57–59; M. Safjan, "Refleksje wokół konstytucyjnych…," p. 227; P. Tuleja, "Stosowanie Konstytucji…," p. 125; L. Bosek, *Gwarancje godności ludzkiej…*, p. 121–124.

absolute character and applies to everyone. But the duty to respect and protect dignity was imposed on public authorities of the state.'[195]

It would seem that, unlike the above-mentioned negative obligations, the one referred to in Art. 31 para. 2 of the Constitution, that is, the obligation to respect the freedoms and rights of others, would be formulated in positive terms. However, we should observe that 'respect' means refraining from interference with the sphere of constitutional rights and freedoms, so in actual fact it also has a negative character and does not entail any obligation for private entities to take any specific positive measures, in particular ones aiming to protect such rights and freedoms. Such an understanding of the notion of 'respect' is confirmed by an analysis of the aforementioned Art. 30 of the Constitution, where the obligations of public authorities with regard to human dignity were described as 'respect and protection,' thus respect was clearly distinguished from protection.

The prohibition of discrimination in social or economic life, referred to in Art. 32 para. 2 of the Constitution, clearly confirms the view that constitutional rights and freedoms may be have private entities as their addressees and that constitutional provisions may introduce negative obligations for such entities. Social and economic life referred to in this provision is clearly contrasted with political life. The former concerns the individual's functioning in the society, that is, his relations with other individuals, while the latter means an individual's functioning in a state being a political organization, hence mainly his relations with public authorities.

Another obligation formulated in positive terms is contained in the aforementioned Art. 72 para. 3 of the Constitution, pursuant to which, in the course of establishing the rights of a child, persons responsible for children, should consider and, as far as possible, give priority to the views of the child. Similarly, the Preamble of the Constitution formulates the obligation of 'solidarity with others,' which is given a universal character. Though it is much less specific than the obligation to consider and, as far as possible, give priority to the views of the child, it is undoubtedly not just a declaration devoid of a normative meaning.

Indirectly, two more positive obligations for private entities result from constitutional provisions. Both consist in the need to take specific measures. One is the obligation to provide information about activities of self-governing economic or professional bodies as well as other persons and organizational units to the extent to which they perform the duties of public authorities and

---

[195] Judgments of the Constitutional Tribunal: of April 11, 2001, Ref. No. K 11/00; of February 24, 2010, Ref. No. K 6/09.

manage communal assets or property of the State Treasury (Art. 61 para. 1 of the Constitution) and the other is the obligation of public organizations and institutions to consider petitions, proposals and complaints in connection with their prescribed duties within the field of public administration (Art. 63 of the Constitution). We should stress that private entities' obligations versus other private entities cannot be implied, while the constitutional provision imposing such obligations must meet certain minimum requirements of specificity, which means in practice that it should identify the legal norm's addressee as well as the scope of its application (hypothesis) and its regulation (disposition).[196]

Summarizing the above reflections, we should state that constitutional provisions introduce mainly negative obligations for private entities, though some of these provisions are also the legal grounds for construing positive obligations.

5.1.6. Consequences of Infringements of Constitutional Rights and Freedoms by Private Entities

The Constitution does not expressly grant to individuals any means for the protection of their rights and freedoms against infringements by private entities, nor does it directly define any legal sanctions[197] for such infringements. We should note that the particularity of constitutional norms means they do not follow the conception of the three components of a legal norm (hypothesis, disposition, sanction),[198] which conception applies in criminal law. Most acts described in the subchapter entitled 'Means for the Defense of Freedoms and Rights' may be used when constitutional rights and freedoms are violated by a public authority. And so, the right to compensation for harm, referred to in Art. 77 para. 1 of the Constitution, applies if the harm is done by 'an organ of public authority contrary to law.' The right to constitutional complaint, as referred to in Art. 79 of the Constitution, concerns an infringement of constitutional freedoms or rights by a normative act on the basis of which

---

[196] K. Wojtyczek, "Horyzontalny wymiar...," p. 231.

[197] In understand the notion of legal sanctions to mean the negative consequences of failure to respect a legal norm. The same approach was adopted by among others, K. Opałek (in:) P. Ehrlich (ed.), *Teoria państwa i prawa*, Warszawa 1957, p. 116–119; J. Filipek, "Jeszcze o sankcji prawnej," *Państwo i Prawo*, 4 (65), p. 633; T. Liszcz, *Nieważność czynności prawnej w umownych stosunkach pracy*, Warszawa 1977, p. 27.

[198] On the three elements of conception of a legal norm *cf.* P. Wronkowska, *Podstawowe pojęcia prawa...*, p. 18.

'a court or organ of public administration has made a final decision.' Even the right to apply to the Ombudsman, expressed in Art. 80 of the Constitution, serves to protect the rights and freedoms infringed by 'organs of public authority.'

Therefore, among the provisions of the subchapter devoted to means of defense of constitutional freedoms and rights, the only one that could be relied upon in case of infringements by private entities are the right of access to court (Art. 77 para. 2 in conjunction with Art. 45 para. 1 of the Constitution). In this case there is no indication of the entity violating the constitutional rights or freedoms, but once there is no clear reservation that this concerns violations by public authorities, we should assume that private entities can commit violations too. According to Krzysztof Wojtyczek, the 'right to protection of the rights of an individual with means of state coercion against violations by private entities could be inferred from the right of access to court. Yet it was left to the legislator to give effect to this right. Thus, enforcing respect for human rights in horizontal relations is completely dependent on the relevant statutes being enacted.'[199] We can, however, question this thesis, because once Art. 77 para. 2 in conjunction with Art. 45 para. 1 of the Constitution applies directly, pursuant to Art. 8 para. 2, then lack of statutory regulation cannot close the judicial path of asserting the constitutional rights or freedoms violated by a private entity. Such an effect is produced only by a statute which positively determines this issue, i.e. one which closes the judicial path in a given case.

The efficiency of the judicial path in horizontal relations depends on the existence of legal sanctions determining the negative consequences of breaching constitutional provisions both for parties of these relations and for the legal existence of actions taken by these parties. Yet the Constitution does not provide for legal sanctions of this kind,[200] hence we should rather look for them in statutory provisions. It results from Art. 31 para. 3 of the Constitution that any limitations in the exercise of constitutional freedoms and rights may be imposed only by statute, and only when necessary in a democratic state, for instance to protect the freedoms and rights of other persons, but without violating the essence of such rights and freedoms. If the legal sanction defines the negative consequences of violations of rights and freedoms in

---

[199] K. Wojtyczek, "Horyzontalny wymiar…," p. 238.

[200] Although we should note the view of P. Kaźmierczyk, pursuant to which the Constitution's sanction is its supreme legal force resulting in derogation. *Cf.* idem, "Sankcja konstytucji jako zagadnienie metodologiczne" (in:) A. Bator (ed.), *Z zagadnień teorii i filozofii prawa. Konstytucja*, Wrocław 1999, p. 18 et. seq.

horizontal relations and if limitations in the enjoyment of constitutional freedoms and rights result from it, then all this needs to be expressed in a statute.

An act in law performed by two private entities in infringement of constitutional provisions may be classified as a defective act.[201] If an act in law is found to be defective, this may give rise to various consequences specified by the law, the most severe of them being the invalidity of this act. But it should be stressed unequivocally that not every defective act in law is invalid. It is invalid only when the law clearly provides so in the given circumstances. This sanction is the most radical one, so the legislator usually links it with the worst cases of defectiveness or with situations which, in its view, deserve special protection.[202]

In both civil and labor law, the sanction of invalidity[203] applies, among other cases, to an act which is contrary to statute, so it should be considered whether it might apply also to infringement of a constitutional provision which establishes certain rights or freedoms. In both cases it is possible to retroactively validate an act in law, which begs the question about the possibility of applying retroactive validation in cases of constitutional rights violations committed by private entities.

Pursuant to Art. 58 § 1 of the Polish Civil Code, an act in law which is contrary to statutory law or aims to circumvent statutory law is invalid unless the pertinent provision anticipates a different consequence, in particular when it inserts the relevant statutory provisions instead of the invalid clauses of an act in law. With respect to agreements, the provision should be read in conjunction with Art. 353[1] of the Civil Code, which expresses the principle of freedom of contract in relations involving obligations. In accordance with the latter provision, when entering into a contract, the parties can shape their legal relation as they think fit, provided that its content or aim is not contrary to the nature of the relation, statutory law or principles of social coexistence. By juxtaposing both these provisions one reaches the conclusion that not every act in law which infringes a statute is invalid, but only the ones whose content or aim are contrary to, or aim to circumvent, statutory law.[204] Not all

---

[201] P. Grzybowski (ed.), *System prawa cywilnego*, t. I, *Część ogólna*, Wrocław–Warszawa–Kraków–Gdańsk 1974, p. 591; J. Preussner-Zamorska, *Nieważność jako postać wadliwości czynności prawnej*, Kraków 1977, p. 17 and p. 45.

[202] T. Liszcz, *Nieważność czynności…*, p. 36. Similarly *cf.* J. Preussner-Zamorska, *Nieważność jako postać…*, p. 69.

[203] About the doubts whether invalidity can be classified as a sanction, *cf.* P. Sobolewski, "Kontrowersje wokół pojęcia nieistnienia i nieważności czynności prawnej," *Przegląd Prawa Handlowego*, 5 (2009), p. 30–31.

[204] M. Gutowski, *Nieważność czynności prawnej*, Warszawa 2012, p. 197–198.

statutory provisions restrict, at the same time, the freedom of contract, but only those that are unconditionally applicable (*ius cogens*) or semi-imperative in nature.[205] The latter kind establishes a minimum scope of protection of interests of one of the parties, so in a contract it is only possible to depart from them when the contractual provisions are more advantageous for the party covered by normative protection.[206]

Both Art. 58 and Art. 353[1] of the Civil Code use the notion of 'statute' as a normative act an infringement of which makes an act in law invalid. But it should be recognized that in both these provisions the statute is a synonym of law in the broad sense, including the Constitution.[207] This gives grounds to state that unconstitutionality of the content or the aim of an act in law makes this act invalid.[208]

The requirement of consistency of the content and the aim of an act in law with the Constitution undoubtedly limits the freedom of contract.[209] The parties cannot create the relation of obligation between them in contraventio of the imperatives and prohibitions expressed in the Constitution. By virtue of Art. 58 of the Civil Code in conjunction with Art. 40 of the Constitution, a contractual clause providing that failure to repay a loan on time can result in the creditor applying corporal punishment will be invalid. Yet it is not only the content, but also the aim, of an act in law that must not be incompatible with the Constitution. The aim of a contract is the state of affairs which the parties strive to achieve and which is agreed by the parties or at least of which they are aware. The aim need not be stated in the contract, but it must be determinable on the basis of circumstances surrounding its conclusion. Also an act in law aiming to circumvent a statute is invalid, pursuant to Art. 58 § 1 of the Civil Code. The notion of 'circumventing the law' is understood as an act not prohibited by law, but undertaken in order to achieve an aim prohibited by the law.[210]

---

[205] M. Safjan, "Zasada swobody umów (Uwagi wstępne na tle wykładni art. 353[1] k.c.)," *Państwo i Prawo*, 4 (1993), p. 14; M. Safjan, "Efekt horyzontalny...," p. 313; Z. Radwański, *Teoria umów*, Warszawa 1977, p. 120.

[206] Z. Radwański, *Teoria umów...*, p. 120.

[207] Z. Kędzia, "Horyzontalne działanie...," przyp. 1, p. 532; K. Wojtyczek, "Horyzontalny wymiar...," p. 239; M. Safjan, "Efekt horyzontalny...," p. 353–355; M. Granat, "W sprawie niektórych kwestii związanych z podpisywaniem przez kandydatów na posłów weksli in blanco," *Przegląd Sejmowy*, 2 (2007), p. 120; M.H. Koziński, "W sprawie oceny ważności niektórych zobowiązań cywilnoprawnych, których skutkiem może być ograniczenie swobody wykonywania mandatu posła i senatora," *Przegląd Sejmowy*, 2 (2007), p. 129.

[208] M. Gutowski, *Nieważność czynności...*, p. 225; Z. Radwański, *Teoria umów...*, p. 117.

[209] M. Gutowski, *Nieważność czynności...*, p. 200.

[210] The author of this definition is A. Wolter; different definitions of the notion of *in fraudem legis* acts were given by e.g. F. Zoll or Z. Radwański. The notion of 'circumvention of the law' is defined similarly by T. Liszcz. *Cf.* T. Liszcz, *Nieważność czynności...*, p. 47.

In principle, the effects of invalidity of an act in law are described in similar ways in jurisprudence[211] and judicature. In its judgment of April 7, 2010, Ref. No. II UK 357/09, the Polish Supreme Court held that the 'invalidity determined under Art. 58 of the Civil Code (…) is absolute, which means that the act in law has not produced and cannot produce any legal effects intended by the parties. This invalidity arises by operation of law and from the very start (*ex tunc*), i.e. from the time when the invalid act in law was performed.'

Therefore, an invalid act in law does not produce legal effects, regardless of the parties' standpoint on the issue.[212] It should be recognized by state authorities *ex officio;* everyone can invoke invalidity which exists objectively, regardless of the intentions of parties to an act in law. Such an act in law is invalid from the moment it is performed, so the act is not deprived of legal effects, but – as it is assumed – does not produce such effects. In other words, an invalid act in law fails to produce the legal effects which the law links with acts of this kind.

The sanction of invalidity exists in labor law, too. Under Art. 18 of the Polish Labor Code, provisions of contracts and acts on whose basis the employment relation was created cannot be less favorable to the employee than provisions of labor law, otherwise they are invalid and the relevant provisions of labor law are applied instead. Similarly, the provisions of contracts and acts on whose basis the employment relation is created must not infringe the principle of equal treatment in employment. These provisions are replaced by the appropriate provisions of labor law and if there are no such provisions of law, they should be replaced by appropriate non-discriminatory provisions. And pursuant to Art. 9 § 2 of the Labor Code, the provisions of collective labor agreements, internal regulations and charters cannot be less favorable to employees than the Labor Code, other statutes and implementing acts. Although in this case the legislator did not expressly introduce the sanction of invalidity, Art. 9 § 4 of the Labor Code does state that those provisions of collective labor agreements and other collective arrangements based on statutory law, internal regulations and charters that set forth the rights and duties of parties of the employment relation which infringe the principle of equal treatment in employment, do not apply. Hence this effect is the same as the effect of the sanction of invalidity.

---

[211] A different definition of 'invalid acts in law' is given by e.g.. T. Gizbert-Studnicki, who claims that 'Invalid acts in law are legal facts and belong to the group of manifestations of intention which are similar to declarations of intention.' *Cf.* idem, "O nieważnych czynnościach prawnych w świetle koncepcji czynności konwencjonalnych," *Państwo i Prawo*, 4 (1975), p. 82.

[212] T. Liszcz, *Nieważność czynności…*, p. 27.

Art. 9 and Art. 18 of the Labor Code set the boundaries of autonomy of intentions of parties to the employment relation.[213] Both these provisions refer to the notion of 'provisions of labor law.' Pursuant to Art. 9 § 1 of the Labor Code, whenever the Labor Code mentions the labor law, this is understood to mean the provisions of the Labor Code and of other statutes and implementing acts which define the rights and duties of employees and employers, as well as the provisions of collective labor agreements and other collective arrangements, internal regulations and charters based on statutory law if they define the rights and duties of parties to an employment relation. This provision omits the Constitution, as well as other sources of universally binding law listed in the Constitution, i.e. ratified international agreements and enactments of local law (Art. 87 of the Constitution), European Union law (Art. 91 para. 3 of the Constitution) or regulations having the force of statute (Art. 234 of the Constitution). If all these normative acts were deemed not to be provisions of labor law determining the relation of employment, this would lead to the conclusion of unconstitutionality of Art. 9 §1 of the Labor Code. Therefore, applying a pro-constitutional interpretation of this provision, one should state that it does not contain an exhaustive list of sources of labor law, but needs to be supplemented with the sources of universally binding law listed in the constitutional provisions. The main aim of this provision is to extend the list of sources of law in the sphere of labor law to include instruments executed by the social partners, i.e. collective labor agreements and other collective arrangements based on statutory law, as well as internal instruments, such as regulations and charters. So there are no obstacles to holding that the sanction of invalidity affects the provisions of employment contracts and other acts on the basis of which the employment relation was established, as well as the provisions of collective labor agreements and other collective arrangements based on statutory law, as well as regulations and charters, which provisions are less favorable for employees than constitutional provisions.

The view concerning the invalidity of contractual provisions incompatible with the Constitution seems to be approved in Polish Constitutional Tribunal's case law too. The cases which seem representative for this line of judicial decisions are those in which the Tribunal held that unconstitutionality of provisions repeated in charters of housing cooperatives resulted in the loss of binding force of the latter. On this occasion it should be stressed that, according to the Tribunal, there are no grounds for 'treating the charter of a housing cooperative as a *quasi*-normative act with a universally binding

---

[213] Judgment of the Supreme Court of July 5, 2005, Ref. No. I PK 276/04.

force.'[214] Thus the Constitutional Tribunal approves the view that the charter of a housing cooperative has the nature of a contract, which is widespread in case law.[215] The Supreme Court accepts that a charter 'is a special kind of a contract'[216] or is 'an act in law whose nature is close to that of a contract,'[217] or even – as it stated in the judgment of March 14, 2008, Ref. No. IV CSK 515/2007 – it is simply a contract concluded by the founders through signing the charter, which should be interpreted in the same way as declarations of intention.[218] Also legal academics approve the view of the contractual character of charters.[219] As a consequence of considering a charter as part of contractual law (*lex contractus*) a whole set of civil law provisions on acts in law[220] apply to it, especially Art. 58 of the Civil Code.

In the judgment of February 25, 1999, Ref. No. K 23/98, the Constitutional Tribunal held that 'recognition of Art. 228 § 3 [of the Act of September 16, 1982 – Cooperative Law] as unconstitutional means unconstitutionality of identical provisions contained in the charters of housing cooperatives. A charter cannot contain regulations which are contrary to universally binding laws, including the Constitution.' This view was then further elaborated in the judgment of March 30, 2004, Ref. No. K 32/03, in which the Constitutional Tribunal held that: 'statutes on cooperatives, while leaving considerable leeway for shaping the relations between the housing cooperative and other entities (members and third parties) in the charter, cannot be treated as permitting the introduction of rules that are contrary to basic constitutional rules or mandatory rules of civil law. Neither a contract, nor a charter, nor a resolution can lead, for instance, to differentiation of entities in a similar situation, which in particular results in unequal (worse) treatment of one of them (prohibition of discrimination), which differentiation is not specifically justified by the system of applicable laws or values of the constitutional order.'

Apart from the sanction of invalidity, the second consequence of infringing constitutional rights and freedoms might be the right holder pursuing

---

[214] *Cf.* judgment of the Constitutional Tribunal of April 13, 1999, Ref. No. K 36/98.

[215] *Cf.* judgments of the Supreme Court: of September 30, 2009, Ref. No. V CSK 86/2009, of November 20, 2002, Ref. No. V CKN 1474/2000; resolution of the Supreme Court of May 23, 1989, Ref. No. III CZP 34/89.

[216] Judgment of the Supreme Court of June 27, 2012, Ref. No. IV CSK 557/2011.

[217] Resolution of the Supreme Court of April 3, 1998, Ref. No. III CZP 5/98.

[218] Also judgment of the Supreme Court of September 17, 2008, Ref. No. III CSK 79/2008.

[219] *Cf.* gloss by K. Pietrzykowski to judgment of the Supreme Court of March 11, 1997, Ref. No. III CKN 34/97.

[220] Judgment of the Court of Appeal in Poznan of October 14, 2003, Ref. No. I ACa 757/2003.

a claim against the beholden in a lawsuit.[221] Discussing all the possible claims is beyond the framework of this book, which is why I shall only mention one: the claim for damages.

Pursuant to Art. 415 of the Civil Code 'Whoever by his own fault causes a damage to another person shall be obliged to redress it.' The condition for liability to pay compensation introduced in this provision is the unlawfulness of the damage, understood as it being contrary to the applicable legal order, so also to the Constitution. In addition, the notion of the legal order in the context of Art. 415 of the Civil Code covers not only the 'imperatives and prohibitions resulting from the legal norm, but also the imperatives and prohibitions resulting from moral and customary norms referred to as "principles of social coexistence" or "good customs." This understanding of the notion of unlawfulness in civil law is broader than the expression "contrary to law" used in Art. 77 para. 1 of the Polish Constitution.'[222] The sanction of compensation may be triggered when the private entity, by a culpable action or omission, infringes the constitutional rights and freedoms of another private entity either by a direct infringement of the constitutional provisions establishing the said rights and freedoms or by an indirect violation of – for instance – principles of social coexistence, whose substance is determined on the basis of constitutional provisions establishing the said rights and freedoms. In both cases, the condition for liability to pay compensation is the damage caused by the private entity's action or omission.

5.1.7. Closing Remarks

The conception of the direct horizontal effect of constitutional rights can be applied under the Polish Constitution, although undoubtedly only in exceptional situations, when constitutional rights are not sufficiently protected at the level of statutes or when statutory protection is redundant in view of its sufficient level accorded in the Constitution.[223] This means that private enti-

---

[221] On the notion of 'claim' cf. P. Wronkowska (in:) A. Redelbach, P. Wronkowska, Z. Ziembiński, *Zarys teorii państwa i prawa*, Warszawa 1992, p. 149; P. Wronkowska (in:) P. Wronkowska, Z. Ziembiński, *Zarys teorii prawa...*, p. 105–106.

[222] *Cf.* judgments of the Supreme Court: of February 19, 2003, Ref. No. V CKN 1681/00; of February13, 2004, Ref. No. IV CK 40/03.

[223] An example of the latter kind of regulation is the prohibition of subjecting individuals to torture and using corporal punishment (Art. 40 of the Constitution), which, formulated unequivocally on the level of constitutional norms, does not need further clarification or, the more so, repetition at the level of statutory norms.

ties can, in certain clearly determined conditions, invoke constitutional rights in horizontal relations and, directly on the basis of constitutional provisions, formulate claims against other private entities. An analysis of the contents of constitutional provisions which enshrine the rights and freedoms of an individual leads to the conclusion that some of them could apply in horizontal relations. Sometimes these provisions can be applied autonomously, because they are sufficiently precise and, moreover, they lack a sufficient 'wrapping' of statutory regulation. Consequently, they can be an autonomous source of claims for infringements of the said rights and freedoms. These provisions grant certain rights to some private entities, while obliging other private entities to refrain from certain behaviors or sometimes to behave in a certain way. Last, but not least, there are sanctions which can be triggered in case of granting the private entity's claim for infringement of his constitutional rights or freedoms by another private entity. These sanctions result from statutory provisions, which use a broad notion of 'infringement of law' covering also infringements of the Constitution.

5.2. The Model of the Indirect Horizontal Effect of Constitutional Rights

5.2.1. Preliminary Remarks

According to the conception of the indirect horizontal effect of constitutional rights, these rights should be taken into account by courts in the process of interpreting and applying normative acts that constitute direct legal grounds for judicial decisions on disputes between private entities. Constitutional rights express certain values and therefore integrate the society around shared ideas.[224] A condition for an indirect horizontal effect of constitutional rights is a proper formulation of statutory provisions, in particular their flexible rendition through application of general clauses and indeterminate phrases.[225] Through them courts can take into account, in their adjudication process, the constitutional rights of parties engaged in a dispute. At the same time, courts must resolve collisions of constitutional rights by balancing the values underlying these rights.[226]

---

[224] Similarly cf. B. Banaszak, "Ogólne wiadomości...," p. 50.
[225] P. Lindenbergh, "Fundamental rights...," p. 374–375.
[226] M. Safjan, "Efekt horyzontalny praw podstawowych...," p. 307.

5.2.2. Characteristics of the Model Based on Examples of States Where it is Applied

The model of the indirect horizontal effect of constitutional rights is applied in Germany[227] and in South Africa.[228] Its basic assumption is that these rights bind the state and entities acting on its behalf. In other words, enforceable obligations of private entities are not to be derived directly from constitutional provisions, unless the provisions of the constitution, such as Art. 9 para. 3 second sentence, of the German Constitution, explicitly so provide.[229] Precisely this view is formulated in Germany based on the content of Art. 1 para. 3 of the German Constitution, according to which basic rights, being directly applicable, are binding upon the legislature, the executive and the judiciary.[230] In South Africa, grounds for this view can be found in the wording of Art. 8 para. 1 of the 1996 Constitution, according to which the Bill of Rights applies to 'all law, and binds the legislature, the executive, the judiciary and all organs of state.'

At the same time, in both countries it is highlighted that constitutional rights are of significance for horizontal relations. In South Africa, this very idea is expressed in Art. 8 para. 2 of the 1996 Constitution, according to which the Bill of Rights 'binds a natural or a juristic person if, and to the extent that, it is applicable, taking into account the nature of the right and the nature of any duty imposed by the right.' No doubt this provision shows that only some of the constitutional rights have horizontal dimension. This provision does not, however, predetermine how the Bill of Rights binds natural and legal

---

[227] H. Linders, *Über der Frage…*, p. 94–95; T. Langer, *Die Problematik der Geltung…*, p. 66; H. Rösler, "Harmonizing the German civil code of the nineteenth century with a modern constitution – the Lüth Revolution 50 years ago in comparative perspective," *Tulane European and Civil Law Forum*, 23 (2008), p. 25.

[228] J. Fedtke, "South Africa. From indirect to direct effect in South Africa: A system in transition" (in:) D. Oliver, J. Fedtke (eds.), *Human Rights and the Private Sphere. A Comparative Study*, New York 2007, p. 353; D. Oliver, J. Fedtke, "Comparative analysis" (in:) D. Oliver, J. Fedtke (eds.), *Human Rights and the Private Sphere*, p. 484; M. Kumm, V. Ferreres Comella, "What is so special about constitutional rights in private litigation? A comparative analysis of the function of state action requirements and indirect horizontal effect" (in:) A. Sajo, R. Uitz (eds.), *The Constitution in Private Relations. Expanding Constitutionalism*, Utrecht 2005, p. 242; F. du Bois, "Private law in the age of rights" (in:) E. Reid, D. Visser (eds.), *Private Law and Human Rights. Bringing Rights Home in Scotland and South Africa*, Edinburgh 2013, p. 13.

[229] G. Dürig (in:) T. Maunz, G. Dürig, R. Herzog, R. Scholz, P. Lerche, H-J. Papier, A. Randelzhofer, E. Schmidt-Assmann, *Grundgesetz. Kommentar, Band I*, Munchen 1990, p. 64.

[230] G. Dürig, "Grundrechte und Zivilrechtsprechung" (in:) T. Maunz (ed.), *Von Bonner Grundgesetz zur gesamtdeutschen Verfassung. Festschrift zum 75. Geburtstag von Hans Nawiasky*, München 1956, p. 176.

persons. It is the following paragraph of this provision, i.e. Art. 8 para. 3, that puts forward the concept of the indirect horizontal effect of constitutional rights. According to its wording, when applying a provision of the Bill of Rights, a court applies, or if necessary develops, the common law to the extent that legislation does not give effect to that right and may develop rules of the common law to limit the right. Moreover, according to Art. 39 para. 2 of the 1996 Constitution of South Africa, when interpreting any legislation, and when developing the common law or customary law, the court must promote the spirit, purport and objects of the Bill of Rights. In Germany, the Constitution does not directly address the problem of the horizontal effect of basic rights. It was the case law of the Federal Constitutional Court that formulated the requirement of interpreting statutory law in a way that respects the basic rights. General clauses and other indeterminate phrases play a key role in the process of this interpretation.[231]

The indirect effect of constitutional rights involves giving them a more tangible dimension in the process of applying the law by courts. In Germany, it is assumed that basic rights manifest the constitutional system of values. This doctrine was developed quite robustly in the post-war case law of the Federal Constitutional Court, beginning with the judgment in the *Lüth* case of 1958,[232] mainly in cases involving limits upon the freedom of expression that remains in collision with the protection of personal rights.[233] The difference versus the doctrine of direct horizontal effect lies in grounds for the individual's claim against another individual being not a provision of the constitution, but of a statute, while during the process of interpreting this provision, the court takes into account the impact that its wording has upon the order of values set by basic rights.[234] Thus, the Federal Constitutional Court formulated a theory of mutual interaction (*Wechselwirkung*) of the Constitution and statutes. Just like statutory provisions influence the basic rights

---

[231] G. Dürig (in:) T. Maunz and others, *Grundgesetz...*, p. 66; G. Dürig, *Grundrechte...*, p. 176; W. Reimers, *Die Bedeutung der Grundrechte...*, p. 16.

[232] Judgment of the Federal Constitutional Court of January 15, 1958, Ref. No. 1 BvR 400/51, BVerfGE 7,198 (*Lüth*).

[233] Judgments of the Federal Constitutional Court: of February 26, 1969, Ref. No. 1 BvR 619/63, BVerfGE 25, 256 (*Blinkfüer*); of June 10, 1964, Ref. No. 1 BvR 37/63, BVerfGE 18, 85 (*Spezifisches Verfassungsrecht*); of February 24, 1971, Ref. No. 1 BvR 435/68, BVerfGE 30, 173 (*Mephisto*); of May 11, 1976, Ref. No. 1 BvR 671/70, BVerfGE 42, 143 (*Deutschland Magazin*); of June 3, 1980, Ref. No. 1 BvR 797/78, BVerfGE 54, 208 (*Böll / Walden*); of January 25, 1984, Ref. No. 1 BvR 272/81, BVerfGE 66, 116 (*Springer / Wallraff*); of February 9, 1994, Ref. No. 1 BvR 1687/92, BVerfGE 90, 27 (*Parabolantenne*).

[234] S. Oeter, "Fundamental rights and their impact on private law – doctrine and practice under the German Constitution," *Tel Aviv University Studies in Law*, 12 (1994), p. 13.

expressed in the Constitution and limit them, thus also these basic rights affect statutory provisions, the general clauses included, and determine their interpretation in a certain manner. The limits of basic rights are also determined by the circumstances of collision of various goods protected by the law and the need to balance these goods. Goods should be balanced *in concreto*, i.e. with regard to all the circumstances of the case.

Transposition of basic rights into the legal system, figuratively termed the 'radiating effect'(*Ausstrahlugswirkung*) takes place in various ways.[235] Initially, the Federal Constitutional Court assumed that it transpired thanks to general clauses only, and subsequently, that it took place also through indeterminate phrases. It is now believed that whenever a private law provision restricts a basic right, the courts that apply this provision should, when resolving a case, have regard for the meaning of the said basic right. Specifically, courts should balance interests protected under the given basic right with interests protected under the private law provision. Such balancing is usually done while establishing the meaning of a phrase contained in a statute of private law or when taking into account the specific circumstances of a case.[236] This approach is named basic rights-oriented interpretation (*grundrechtsorientierte Auslegung, grundrechtsorientierte Abwägung*) or interpretation consistent with basic rights (*grundrechtskonforme Auslegung*).

In South Africa, the need to have regard for constitutional rights has been explicitly imposed upon courts in the 1996 Constitution.[237] Its Art. 8 para. 3 provides that when applying a provision of the Bill of Rights to a natural or juristic person, in order to give effect to a right in the Bill, a court must apply, or if necessary develop, the common law to the extent that legislation does not give effect to that right, and may develop rules of the common law to limit the right, provided that the limitation is in accordance with Art. 36 para. 1 of the 1996 Constitution. Hence, the constitutional right binds an individual (imposes obligations upon an individual), yet it is applied only when it is embodied in normative acts or in the common law. Thus, a court would first examine whether a given right is implemented in normative acts, and if not – whether it is provided for in the common law, and unless so found, develops the common law by creating a rule that gives effect to this right. The

---

[235] P. Egli, *Drittwirkung von Grundrechten…*, p. 23.

[236] R. Brinktrine, „The horizontal effect of human rights in German constitutional law: The British debate on horizontality and the possible role model of the German doctrine of 'mittelbare Drittwirkung der Grundrechte'," *European Human Rights Law Review*, 4 (2001), p. 424.

[237] Judgments of the Constitutional Court of South Africa: of May 15, 1996, Ref. No. CCT 8/95 (*du Plessis v. de Klerk*), ZACC 10 (1996); of June 14, 2002, Ref. No. CCT 53/01 (*Kumalo v. Holomisa*), ZACC 12 (2002).

jurisprudence points that in the circumstances, where the common law does not endow an individual with legal grounds for asserting his rights before a court, such grounds should be created by the court by way of an appropriate development of the common law.[238]

Since the model of the indirect horizontal effect of constitutional rights assigns a key role to courts, which have the duty to have regard for basic rights in the process of resolving disputes between private parties, hence the aspect of reviewing their activity is of major significance. In Germany this problem was repeatedly examined by the Federal Constitutional Court which emphasized that matters such as evidentiary court hearing, findings and assessment of facts, interpretation of statutory provisions and their application in the given case fall within the competence of common courts and are beyond the scope of review of the Federal Constitutional Court.[239] The latter may interfere only when a court violates a specific basic right; however, not every such violation justifies its interference. Violation of a basic right that does justify interference by the Federal Constitutional Court takes place when a judge is either obviously unaware that basic rights should influence his decision or has a wrong perception of the importance and scope of protection of basic rights, which in turn affects the outcome of the case. It is not sufficient for the assumption that basic rights have been violated if the judge, when applying the statutory general clauses, balances colliding interests of the parties in a debatable way by giving too much or too little weight to certain rights.

5.2.3. Transposition of Constitutional Values into Private Law as a Result of the Direct Application of the Polish Constitution

5.2.3.1. Basic Assumptions of the Constitutional Values Radiating Effect

Positivization of axiology, i.e. transposing values into the content of legal norms takes place above all at the constitutional level. If we were to accept the premise that I share, namely that constitutional rights have their origin in

---

[238] J. van der Walt, "Progressive indirect horizontal application of the bill of rights: towards a co-operative relation between common-law and constitutional jurisprudence," *South African Journal on Human Rights*, 17 (2001), p. 354; H. Cheadle, "Third party effect in the South African Constitution" (in:) A. Sajó, R. Uitz (eds.), *The Constitution in private relations. Expending Constitutionalism*, Utrecht 2005, p. 75–76; H. Cheadle, D. Davis, "The application of the 1996 Constitution in the private sphere," *South African Journal on Human Rights* 13 (1997), p. 61.

[239] Judgment of June 10, 1964, Ref. No. 1 BvR 37/63, BVerfGE 18, 85 – *Spezifisches Verfassungsrecht*.

the natural law, their incorporation into the text of the Constitution is tantamount with having its text saturated with values underlying these rights. The values, including those which I have termed 'constitutional values,' are thus of non-constitutional, or even supra-constitutional lineage, according to the theory of the natural law. Their positivization at the constitutional level opens up the possibility of their radiating onto the entire legal system, including private law. This radiating effect takes place primarily through general clauses and evaluative phrases. When applying them in the process of adjudicating in disputes between private parties, courts must refer to constitutional axiology, to which these general clauses and evaluative phrases refer, including the axiology underlying constitutional rights.

The mechanism of indirect effect of constitutional rights upon horizontal relations (their radiating effect) finds perfect conditions to flourish in the Polish legal system. On the one hand, as I have mentioned earlier, the Polish Constitution is saturated with axiology, which is particularly clear in those of its provisions that relate to the rights and freedoms of an individual, for it is these provisions that most frequently refer to the natural law origin of constitutional axiology. As stated in Art. 30 of the Constitution, 'inherent and inalienable dignity of the person' constitutes a source of freedoms and rights of persons and citizens. In turn, the Preamble to the Constitution points to diversification of sources of constitutional axiology, referring both to Christian values as well as universal values (pan-human values). The idea of protecting rights and freedoms enshrined across the Constitution is based on the idea of specific values that lie at their core. Therefore, while regulating aspects relating to a given right or freedom, the legislator must take into account its underlying values. The authorities that apply the law refer to these values when interpreting statutory laws containing general clauses and other indeterminate phrases.[240] A large number of such kind of provisions in the Polish law guarantees some sort of continuity of the radiating effect of constitutional rights and constitutional values onto the system of private law.

5.2.3.2. The Role of General Clauses and Other Indeterminate Phrases

A substantial quantity of general clauses and other indeterminate phrases is a characteristic element of not only the Polish law, but of modern private law in general, regardless of which country is being referred to. At present, it is

---

[240] The terms 'undefined phrases' and 'vague phrases' are also used in the jurisprudence. The term 'undefined phrase' is used alongside the concept of a 'general clause' in § 155 para. 1 of the volume describing principles of legislative techniques 'Zasady techniki prawodawczej.'

not possible, let alone desirable, to construe a system of normative acts without employing a language that opens up this system to values, including those values underlying the constitutional provisions that regulate the rights and freedoms of an individual.[241] This type of language requires of those in charge of singular legal decisions 'cognitive or axiological relativization beyond the system, that is, recourse to the facts or values that have not been incorporated into the legal system.'[242] This opening up of the legal system implies that the authority applying the law must reach beyond this system based on powers afforded to this authority under the system itself.

A characteristic feature of general clauses and other such phrases is the indeterminacy[243] of their content, which leaves to the authorities applying the law – as intended by the legislator – a significant margin of discretion with regard to decision-making.[244] The use of these linguistic phrases is an exception to the principle of drafting statutory provisions so as to express the intentions of the legislator accurately and clearly for the addressees of the norms contained therein.[245] These phrases endow the legislative text with a timeless content, ensure a decision-making margin to authorities applying the law and make it possible to avoid excessive casuistry.[246]

Amongst indeterminate phrases, special role is played by general clauses that can be divided into two types. The first type comprises indeterminate phrases referring to norms and principles derived from extralegal normative systems, such as the principles of social coexistence or equitable principles.[247] Such general clause permits the courts to rely, in the spirit of constitutional axiology, upon extralegal norms, specifically, upon norms relating to morals

---

[241] In the deliberations contained in this chapter, I will refer to studies on general clauses, the results of which I have published. *Cf.* M. Florczak-Wątor, "Kontrola konstytucyjności klauzul generalnych," *Przegląd Sejmowy*, 4 (2013), p. 49–64.

[242] L. Leszczyński, "Konstrukcje otwarte tekstu prawnego wobec zmian społecznych" (in:) H. Rot (ed.), *Prawo i prawoznawstwo wobec zmian społecznych*, Wrocław 1990, p. 76.

[243] Here I mean widely understood indeterminacy, which, however, should be distinguished from distortion. As stated by M. Zieliński, indeterminacy relates to the meaning of phrases, while distortion to their scope. Since these clauses are closely interrelated, hence distortion is often regarded by legal scholars as a kind of indeterminate nature (indeterminacy as to scope), which is distinguished from conceptual indeterminacy. *Cf.* M. Zieliński, *Wykładnia prawa. Zasady, reguły, wskazówki*, Warszawa 2002, p. 180.

[244] K. Wójcik, "Klauzule generalne a zmiany społeczne" (in:) H. Rot (ed.), *Prawo i prawoznawstwo wobec zmian społecznych*, Wrocław 1990, p. 108.

[245] § 6 of the volume describing principles of legislative techniques 'Zasady techniki prawodawczej.'

[246] J. Kaczor, "Z problematyki klauzul generalnych…," p. 162.

[247] On aspects of the principles of social co-existence, *cf.* judgments of the Constitutional Tribunal: of October 17, 2000, Ref. No. SK 5/99; of October 23, 2006, Ref. No. SK 42/04.

or customary conduct.[248] The second type of general clauses are evaluative phrases, indirectly referring to a specific system of values, based on which evaluation is to be made and a decision is to be taken. An example of such phrases include 'the interests of the justice system,'[249] 'undue benefits'[250] or 'manifestly unfounded application.'[251] The concepts of 'interests', 'undue' or 'unfounded' used in these phrases can be analyzed only in the context of a specific axiological system that distinguishes good from evil, fair from unfair, and the founded from the unfounded. These types of general clauses point to the need of weighing, by the court, of certain facts and their specific classification. This division is non-disjunctive by nature, since there exist examples of general clauses that meet the criteria of both these groups, such as the good conduct clause. On the one hand, it involves reliance on a certain system of extralegal norms, and on the other hand, it is a phrase that needs evaluating in terms of representing good or bad conduct.

Thus, what defines a general clause is its indeterminacy and reference to the extralegal system. A general clause may contain references both to a system of norms as well as to a system of values, whereas in both these cases these criteria are extralegal and constitute the measure of evaluation by the authority that applies the law.[252] When using clauses classified under the first group, the authority first concretizes the content of the extralegal norms and principles to which these clauses refer, and then evaluates the examined case in their light. Thus, these extralegal norms and principles complement the legal grounds for a ruling which is generally based on legal norms. It should be noted that a general clause most often carries a specific axiological tint, which is exposed by the legislator already in its naming (for instance good conduct, rules of fair trading). Therefore, general clauses do not rely on just any extralegal norms, but on those falling within a certain axiological framework.[253] In the case of clauses belonging to the second group, this axiomatic context is more noticeable. The authority using this type of clauses first establishes an appropriate system of values, and then, in its light, evaluates whether the facts examined under a particular case fall within its framework. The system of

---

[248] Judgment of the Constitutional Tribunal of July 8, 2008, Ref. No. P 36/07.

[249] Judgment of the Constitutional Tribunal of February 19, 2008, Ref. No. P 48/06.

[250] Judgment of the Constitutional Tribunal of July 8, 2008, Ref. No. P 36/07.

[251] Judgment of the Constitutional Tribunal of October 27, 2010, Ref. No. K 10/08.

[252] According to J. Górski, 'a general clause allows introducing an external evaluative criterion into the legal system.' *Cf.* idem, "Aksjologiczne przesłanki decyzji sądowych w sprawach gospodarczych" (in:) K. Pałecki (ed.), *Dynamika wartości w prawie*, Kraków 1997, p. 144.

[253] *Cf.* judgment of the Supreme Court of January 12, 1999, Ref. No. I CKN 971/97; of October 14, 1998, Ref. No. II CKN 928/97.

values on which the said clause relies allows both to establish the meaning of indeterminate phrases being a part of the clause (for instance, what is meant by 'negligence,' and when such negligence becomes 'gross'), as well to assign them to a specific norm in a particular case (that is, to find whether it is a case of 'gross negligence').

It should be emphasized, however, that such an understanding of general clauses as the one outlined above, is not commonly accepted in the jurisprudence. According to the dominant view, a general clause is not a provision, but a phrase contained therein.[254] However, as rightly pointed out by Z. Ziembiński, 'it would be the most appropriate to use a descriptive phrase that a certain provision contains a general clause, since an evaluative phrase as such is not a general clause, but it gains such attributes only in the context of a specific provision.'[255] There is also a relative uniformity of views as to the general clause being an indeterminate phrase, yet fundamental discrepancies focus around what may be its point of reference.[256] It is said that a general clause contains reference to 'a set of extralegal norms,'[257] 'evaluative and

---

[254] K. Wójcik, „Klauzule generalne a pojęcia prawne i prawnicze (zasady prawa i społeczne niebezpieczeństwo czynu)," *Studia Prawno-Ekonomiczne*, XLV (1990), p. 65; J. Nowacki, "Problem blankietowości przepisów zawierających klauzule generalne" (in:) G. Skąpska and others (eds.), *Prawo w zmieniającym się społeczeństwie. Księga Jubileuszowa Profesor Marii Boruckiej-Arctowej*, Kraków 1992, p. 128; L. Leszczyński, „Właściwości posługiwania się klauzulami generalnymi w prawie prywatnym. Perspektywa zmiany trendu," *Kwartalnik Prawa Prywatnego*, 3 (1995), p. 289; T. Zieliński, "Klauzule generalne w demokratycznym państwie prawnym," *Studia Iuridica*, XXIII (1992), p. 137; T. Zieliński, *Klauzule generalne w prawie pracy*, Warszawa 1988, p. 47; A. Góralczyk-Papoń, "Klauzule generalne w prawie cywilnym – zagrożenie dla porządku prawnego, czy instrument dostosowawczy prawa do zmiennych warunków gospodarczych?," *Humanistyczne Zeszyty Naukowe – Prawa Człowieka*, 7 (2000), p. 159; Z. Radwański, M. Zieliński, "Uwagi *de lege ferenda* o klauzulach generalnych w prawie prywatnym," *PLeg*, 2 (2001), p. 11–12; E. Rott-Pietrzyk, "Klauzule generalne rozsądku w kodeksie cywilnym," *Kwartalnik Prawa Prywatnego*, 3 (2005), p. 625; M. Safjan, „Klauzule generalne w prawie cywilnym (przyczynek do dyskusji)," *Państwo i Prawo*, 11 (1990), p. 48, note 2; J. Kaczor, "Z problematyki klauzul generalnych…," p. 156.

[255] Z. Ziembiński, "Stan dyskusji nad problematyką klauzul generalnych," *Państwo i Prawo*, 3 (1989), p. 16.

[256] Z. Ziembiński, *Etyczne problemy prawoznawstwa*, Wrocław 1972, p. 160; A. Stelmachowski, "Znaczenie klauzuli generalnej zawartej w art. 386 k.c. w obrocie uspołecznionym," *Przegląd Ustawodawstwa Gospodarczego*, 6 (1968), p. 478; J. Czarzasty, "Przyczynek do problematyki klauzul generalnych," *Państwo i Prawo*, 5 (1978), p. 86; H. Groszyk, L. Leszczyński, "Wartości pozaprawne w procesie…," p. 59; Z. Radwański, M. Zieliński, "Uwagi de lege ferenda o klauzulach…," p. 16; M. Safjan, "Klauzule generalne…," p. 48; T. Zieliński, "Klauzule generalne w demokratycznym…," p. 193.

[257] J. Czarzasty, "Przyczynek do problematyki…," p. 90.

generally-oriented extralegal criteria,'[258] 'extralegal rules and assessments.'[259] Some scholars note, however, that 'There can be no mention of reference to extralegal criteria, based on which the authority applying the law should resolve the given case, since such evaluations are not formulated anywhere. It is only this authority that based on the phrases contained in the provision and relating to extralegal criteria, is to formulate such an assessment after the evaluation process.'[260] Hence, other views can also be found that the 'clause points to certain extralegal values as the criteria for evaluative judgments made by the authority applying the law'[261] or that the assessments made on these grounds are '"entangled in axiology," since applying general clauses forces their interpreter to engage in a valuation.'[262]

The problem of a clear differentiation between general clauses and other indeterminate phrases seems insolvable. While there is no doubt that general clauses are phrases that contain references to extralegal systems of values, such as principles of social coexistence, such doubts will always remain with regard to other indeterminate phrases. Each such phrase requires an assessment by the authority applying the law, which would more or less involve the axiology. It is only intuitively that we accept that phrases indisputably containing an evaluative component, such as 'valid reasons,' 'gross negligence,' or 'substantiated case' are general clauses. Equally intuitively we would not expand the notion of a general clause to include indeterminate phrases with a hardly perceptible axiological tint, which should be consistently understood and applied, regardless of the specific features of the case, namely phrases such as 'guilt,' 'normal consequences of an act or omission' or 'proper performance of duties.'[263] Between these two extremes there exist numerous indeterminate phrases, the classification of which into the group of general clauses is disputable. Nonetheless, jurisprudence makes more or less success-

---

[258] L. Leszczyński, "Praworządne stosowanie prawa a klauzule generalne," *Państwo i Prawo*, 11 (1989), p. 56.

[259] T. Zieliński, *Klauzule generalne w prawie…*, p. 56. Similarly *cf.* W. Jakimowicz, *Publiczne prawa podmiotowe*, Kraków 2002, p. 101–102.

[260] J. Kaczor, "Z problematyki klauzul generalnych…," p. 156.

[261] Ibidem, p. 159

[262] J. Kaczor, "Z problematyki klauzul generalnych…," p. 159; K. Wójcik, "Klauzule generalne a pojęcia…," p. 66; K. Wójcik, "Teoretyczna konstrukcja klauzuli generalnej," *Studia Prawno-Ekonomiczne*, VLIV (1990), p. 58.

[263] It should be noted, however, that in its judgment of June 22, 2010, the Constitutional Tribunal decided that the following phrase is a general clause: 'facilitates the commission of this offense in other similar manner.'

ful attempts to delimit general clauses and other indeterminate phrases.[264] Going further into these terminological distinctions does not seem purposeful from the point of view of further reflections. Given that the mechanism of endowing general clauses and other indeterminate phrases with substance is, as a rule, identical, their precise delineation does not seem to be of any major significance.

No doubt the use by the legislator of general clauses and other indeterminate phrases causes saturation of statutory law with axiology and sort of 'opens up' the law to values.[265] Among these values, there are also ones underlying constitutional rights and freedoms of an individual. Through general clauses and indeterminate phrases, these values permeate into statutory law and affect the way it is understood and applied. As remarked by Andrzej Stelmachowski, 'There is a constant "interflow" between legal norms and norms relating to morals or customary conduct (...). General clauses very often constitute (...) a bridge, a connector between legal norms and a wide spectrum of extralegal norms.'[266] Thus, general clauses and indeterminate phrases facilitate overcoming the text-oriented approach to law which is deeply rooted in our legal culture.[267]

General clauses permit applying legal norms to facts which the legislator could not have predicted in advance due to their exceptional oddity or the emergence of new circumstances. In fact the legislator is not capable of anticipating in the legal provisions and precisely providing for all the potential circumstances, particularly taking into account the complexity of socio-economic environment, the dynamics of its changes and the time horizon of normative acts. For the general clauses to fulfill the tasks assigned to them, their content must each and every time be drafted with due regard for the changes in the 'environment' surrounding the normative act.[268] These chang-

---

[264] Cf. J. Kaczor, "Z problematyki klauzul generalnych...," p. 156. Differently T. Zieliński, *Klauzule generalne w prawie...*, p. 69–85; Z. Radwański, M. Zieliński, "Uwagi de lege ferenda...," p. 13; W. Jakimowicz, *Publiczne prawa...*, p. 104.

[265] E. Łętowska, "Interpretacja a subsumpcja zwrotów niedookreślonych i nieostrych," *Państwo i Prawo*, 7–8 (2011), p. 17; A. Kunicki, "Art. 3 p.o.p.p. de lege ferenda," *Państwo i Prawo*, 9 (1960), p. 975; L. Leszczyński, "Funkcje klauzul odsyłających a model ich tworzenia w systemie prawa," *Państwo i Prawo*, 7 (2000), p. 4; W. Jakimowicz, *Publiczne prawa...*, p. 101.

[266] A. Stelmachowski, "Klauzule generalne w kodeksie cywilnym (Zasady współżycia społecznego – społeczno-gospodarcze przeznaczenie prawa)," *Państwo i Prawo*, 1 (1965), p. 5–6.

[267] E. Łętowska, "Bariery naszego myślenia o prawie w perspektywie integracji z Europą," *Państwo i Prawo*, 4–5 (1996), p. 45.

[268] K. Wójcik, "Klauzule generalne a zmiany...," p. 108.

es should find their reflection in the manner of interpreting and applying general clauses and – in a wider perspective – in the legal regulation with such in-built clauses. Proper application of these normative structures allows the law to keep up with changes taking place in the real world, although legislative amendments tend to fall behind changes taking place in their 'environment.' This ability to render the legal text more flexible through general clauses is an effect of their connection with the extralegal environment, to which they refer. Any change in that environment must trigger a change in the content of a general clause, which change is determined in the process of applying the said clause.

5.2.3.3. Co-Application of the Constitution and Statutes as a Method of Endowing General Clauses and Other Indeterminate Phrases with Contents

The content of general clauses and other indeterminate phrases should be endowed with contents by the authorities applying the law through a method of co-application of the constitution and the statutory law. The constitutional provisions on the rights of individuals in fact contain rooted values that need to be taken into account while interpreting and applying statutory provisions containing a general clause or another indeterminate phrase. The technique of co-application of the constitution and the statutory law can be applied in such cases when aspects that require regard for a specific right of an individual are regulated, in varying degrees and scope, in both these normative acts. Then, as stated by the Constitutional Tribunal in its judgment of November 28, 2001, Ref. No. K 36/01, 'the constitutional provision either, together with a provision of statutory law, turns into a building block for construing a legal norm (which is, however, possible only when the provision is sufficiently specific and precise), or becomes a determinant of the method for establishing the legal meaning of the statutory provision (and thus takes the form of the so-called "interpretation of the statute" in accordance with the Constitution and may take place based on the general constitutional principles).' This type of the direct application of the Constitution may, as already mentioned, have an ornamental, interpretative or modifying character.[269]

Ornamental co-application of the Constitution occurs when the statutory provision is the proper legal grounds for the adjudication, while the constitutional provision is only quoted as a supporting argument or as confirmation

---

[269] L. Garlicki, "Bezpośrednie stosowanie konstytucji…," p. 24; W. Kręcisz, "Stanowisko sądów powszechnych…," p. 66–67; P. Waldziński, "Stosowanie Konstytucji w orzecznictwie…," p. 372.

of the correct direction of interpretation. Application of this technique by courts, despite its certainly educational value, is irrelevant from the point of view of the horizontal effect of constitutional rights. Naturally, it can be argued that also here the constitutional provision somehow determines the legal grounds for adjudication as it provides some interpretational guidance, nonetheless if its application is ornamental by nature, then its omission in the process of applying the law would not affect the final ruling.

In the case of an interpretative co-application of the Constitution and statutes, the constitutional provision determines the manner of understanding the statutory provision. The proper legal grounds for adjudication are found in the statutory provision, the contents of which are determined based on constitutional provision. This technique of the co-application of the Constitution and the statutory law is used when different interpretations of a statutory provision are possible, while it most often occurs as a result of general clauses or indeterminate phrases being in-built into the said provision. Once these normative structures are endowed with substance through appropriate interpretive measures, the statutory provision gains an unambiguous and specific content. Thus, constitutional rights and freedoms must be taken into account by courts when interpreting statutory provisions, particularly those that contain general clauses and indeterminate phrases.

On the other hand, the aim of the modifying co-application is to 'rescue' the constitutionality of a statutory provision by ascribing to it a meaning which makes it consistent with the Constitution. In this way the understanding of a statutory provision is modified compared to the understanding determined on the basis of traditional methods of interpretation. The limit for this practice is, however, the linguistic meaning of the given phrase. Interpretation consistent with the constitution cannot thus overcome the unequivocal result of linguistic interpretation. This modification of the earlier understanding of the statutory provision is achieved by endowing general clauses and indeterminate phrases in this provision with a different substance. In such case, this content is determined taking into account constitutional values, including those underlying constitutional rights and freedoms. If the earlier interpretation of this statutory provision did not take into account these constitutional values, then the application of this technique will unavoidably modify its former understanding.

5.2.3.4. The Court as the Authority Transposing Constitutional Values into Private Law

Bearing in mind that general clauses and other indeterminate phrases need to be 'filled with contents,' there arises a question who and how should do so. Definitely the contents of general clauses and indeterminate phrases cannot be made precise *in abstracto* by the legislator, since this would have been contrary to the purpose of these normative structures.[270] The legislator deliberately uses these phrases in order to leave freedom to the authorities applying the law to concretize them with reference to the merits of the adjudicated case,[271] for these are phrases which, given a cultural context, permit a different understanding of their contents. Thus, instead of embedding a rigid evaluative component within a provision, the legislator shifts the duty to make such an evaluation upon the authority applying the law, at the same time giving it the tools for case-specific evaluation.[272] The legislator can only outline certain general criteria, which the evaluation should follow, yet the legislator itself – instead of the authorities applying the law – cannot perform such an evaluation.[273]

Authorities endow the content of general clauses with substance through axiological choices in the process of applying the law.[274] It is the independent courts that are the most predisposed to endow general clauses and other indeterminate phrases with substance rooted in constitutional values.[275] At least three arguments can be put forward in support of this thesis. Firstly, the courts – unlike the executive branch – are bound only by the Constitution and the statutory law. This means not only that courts may not ignore the statutory law, but that when applying the said law, they must bear in mind the constitutional axiology. Secondly, given their attribute of independence, the courts enjoy a greater freedom of interpretation and, consequently, have

---

[270] Such approach was adopted by the Constitutional Tribunal in its judgment of October 27, 2010, Ref. No. K 10/08, by stating that 'specification in a general manner of even the subjective, objective or the temporary aspect of being manifestly unfounded is contrary to the purpose of the "manifestly unfounded" clause within the framework of judicial procedures.' It should be added here that the Tribunal may not replace the authority applying the law in the process of filling the contents of a general clause with contents.

[271] It refers to the circumstances of the so-called 'intended interpretative margin of freedom,' referred to, *inter alia*, by J. Wróblewski. *Cf.* ibidem, "Tworzenie prawa a wykładnia prawa," *Państwo i Prawo*, 6 (1978), p. 16 *et. seq.*

[272] E. Rott-Pietrzyk, "Klauzule generalne...," p. 625; L. Leszczyński, "Funkcje klauzul odsyłających...," p. 10.

[273] E. Łętowska, "Interpretacja a subsumcja...," p. 22–23.

[274] Ibidem, p. 17.

[275] Judgment of the Constitutional Tribunal of May 8, 2006, Ref. No. P 18/05.

a greater capacity to take into account constitutional values in the process of interpretation. Thirdly, the courts are authorities that are naturally predestined to adjudge on rights and freedoms of an individual, and therefore the duty to take these rights and freedoms into account while adjudicating on disputes between private entities rests with the courts.

5.2.3.5. Controlling the Manner of Transposing Constitutional Values into Private Law

Leaving the freedom to endow general clauses and indeterminate phrases with contents to the authorities applying the law raises the question about the potential control over the proper functioning of this mechanism. For a citizen, the predictability of how the content of a general clause or an indeterminate phrase will be concretized against the circumstantial background of his case and thus, of the outcome of the adjudication process, is of particular importance. In this context, the Polish Constitutional Tribunal refers to the requirement of predictability of the 'lines of evaluation' in the process of using such linguistic phrases.[276] Such predictability exists, according to the Tribunal, when there is a stable set of criteria developed in judicature, according to which general clauses are to be applied. It should be noted here that the concept of a general clause triggers a certain conflict of evaluations on the part of the authority applying the law. On the one hand, it allows adapting the law to the specifics of the given circumstances, thus favoring diversity of evaluations dependent upon a subjective viewpoint of the judge. On the other hand, for reasons of stability and predictability, it commands using general clauses in a manner which is subject to control, which in turn would be an argument in favor of uniform evaluation under similar circumstances, depending on objective criteria binding the judge during the evaluation process. It is therefore a question of how far the freedom of the authority that endows a general clause with contents goes and to what extent this freedom can be subject to limitations and control. In the case of using general clauses which contain references to a system of extralegal norms (such as the principles of social coexistence), a greater objectification of evaluation is required. In contrast, in the case of clauses which contain references to an extralegal system of values (such as, for instance, 'gross negligence'), the room for subjectivity in the evaluation is much larger. The Polish Constitutional Tribunal

---

[276] Judgment of the Constitutional Tribunal of October 17, 2000, Ref. No. SK 5/99. Similarly cf. judgments of the Constitutional Tribunal: of December 4, 2000, Ref. No. P 8/00; of April 15, 2003, Ref. No. SK 4/02; of December 16, 2003, Ref. No. SK 34/03.

highlights that 'the requirement of predictability of the court's ruling when applying a general clause can be dispensed with under three circumstances. First, if the premises for understanding that general clause were not only objective, but also subjective in nature. Secondly, if the content of that general clause failed to pose sufficient guarantees that its adjudicative interpretation will become uniform and precise, so the ability to predict the specific end result is assured. Thirdly, if the law-making powers of court could be derived from the wording of that general clause, expressed in particular in the court's authority to autonomously endow [the provision containing the general clause] with new contents.'[277]

Predictability of judicial decisions made on the basis of provisions containing general clauses and other indeterminate phrases, and thus legal certainty longed for by citizens, raises the need to objectify the judge's evaluation.[278] As remarked by M. Safjan, 'Aiming at full objectification of evaluations seems to defy the very essence of general clauses, depriving them of (...) the needed flexibility and relativity. Grossly subjectivized approaches clash with the postulate of legal certainty, with verifiability of evaluations formulated in the process of its application, leading in effect to haphazardness, thus threatening, at least potentially, the autonomy of acting individuals.'[279] The attempts at juridization of concepts contained in general clauses seem equally purposeless, since the meaning of these concepts is not to be sought in the norms of positive law only. In fact, extralegal references are the essence of a general clause. Although a general clause is incorporated in a legal provision, yet from its name alone one cannot extract specific evaluations, norms and rules of expected behavior.[280] The latter are placed beyond the legal system with all the resultant consequences, particularly uncertainties as to their specific substance.

This does not mean, however, that the adjudicating authority is free to select extralegal norms and values to which the general clause refers. The substance of general clauses should be concretized by the authority applying the law with regard to the fundamental principles of law, values applicable across the system and constitutionally protected standards.[281] A general clause cannot therefore refer to a normative or axiological system that as a rule lies

---

[277] Judgments of the Constitutional Tribunal: of October 17, 2000, Ref. No. SK 5/99; of November 22, 2005, Ref. No. SK 8/05; of October 23, 2006, Ref. No. SK 42/04.

[278] P. Grzybowski, "Struktura i treść przepisów prawa cywilnego odsyłających do zasad współżycia społecznego," *Studia Cywilistyczne*, VI (1965), p. 50; J. Czarzasty, "Przyczynek do problematyki...," p. 92; J. Kaczor, "Z problematyki klauzul...," p. 162.

[279] M. Safjan, "Klauzule generalne...," p. 54. Similarly *cf.* J. Kaczor, "Z problematyki klauzul...," p. 167.

[280] Ibidem.

[281] Judgment of the Constitutional Tribunal of October 27, 2010, Ref. No. K 10/08.

beyond the framework set by the Constitution. The use of general clauses in a democratic country must satisfy the requirements of the rule of law.[282] On the plane of the so-called formal understanding of the rule of law, the use of general clauses requires an explicit consent of the legislator, which is deemed granted when the provision contains such a clause. In turn, in accordance with the substantive understanding of the rule of law, the use of general clauses must take place with respect for universally recognized values, which are protected by the law. As mentioned by T. Zieliński in the context of distinguishing these two meanings of the concept of the rule of law, 'The use of general clauses, just like the law in general, is not possible in isolation from the system of values and evaluations that give the law a certain face, predetermine a social prestige of this law and are the basis for its approval by citizens.'[283] In the conclusion, the same author finds: 'Thus, it is not the formal motivation for the use of a general clause (statutory reference) alone that decides about the lawfulness of a judicial decision based on the given clause, but respect for those extralegal criteria [which the clause refers to] that determines the manner and limits of using these clauses.'[284] A similar view is promoted by K. Wójcik, who claims that 'axiological choices associated with determining the contents of a general clause should (...) fall within a certain axiological framework, set above all by the fundamental valuating assumptions of the entire legal system and expressed, amongst others, in legal principles, binding interpretative guidelines, often also containing general clauses.'[285] Therefore, the use of general clauses may not violate the axiological foundations of the legal order (particularly principles of law that require the protection of certain types of values).[286]

As a minimum for correctness of adjudication by the adjudicating authority, M. Safjan points to the 'need to respect, in the process of applying the law, the fundamental and permanent values rooted in the culture and traditions of a given society, in our case, primarily the values of the Christian culture. Only within a framework so defined, is there room for the "subjectivity of a judge."'[287]

---

[282] For formal and substantive understanding of the rule of law, cf. J. Nowacki, *Praworządność. Wybrane problemy teoretyczne*, Warszawa 1977; J. Kaczor, "Z problematyki klauzul...," p. 160–161; L. Leszczyński, "Praworządne stosowanie prawa...," p. 56–57.

[283] T. Zieliński, *Klauzule generalne w prawie...*, p. 136. Similarly cf. W. Jakimowicz, *Publiczne prawa...*, p. 101.

[284] T. Zieliński, *Klauzule generalne w prawie...*, p. 137.

[285] K. Wójcik, "Klauzule generalne a zmiany...," p. 111.

[286] Z. Ziembiński, "Stan dyskusji nad problematyką...," p. 24.

[287] M. Safjan, "Klauzule generalne...," p. 54. Similarly cf. T. Zieliński, *Klauzule generalne w prawie...*, p. 25; A. Góralczyk-Papoń, "Klauzule generalne...," p. 164.

5.2.3.6. Closing Remarks

The conception of the indirect horizontal effect of constitutional rights is closely related with interpretation and application of constitutional and sub-constitutional norms. It assumes the protection of individual's rights in horizontal relations by introducing general clauses and other indeterminate phrases into statutory law, and endowing these clauses with contents by courts based on values decoded from constitutional norms. These values are taken into account in the process of co-applying the constitution and statutory provisions.

The model of the indirect horizontal effect of constitutional rights seems to best match the specifics of Poland's legal order. Constitutional norms are in fact saturated with axiology, while general clauses and other indeterminate phrases are often used in statutes. Therefore, courts are well placed to have regard for the constitutional axiology while adjudicating in disputes between private entities that, as a rule, are based on statutory norms.[288] These norms are, however, co-applied together with the Constitution, and thus values derived from the latter normative act are taken into account by courts in the adjudication process. The technique of co-applying the Constitution and statutes has been applied in the case law of the Constitutional Tribunal and is accepted by courts.

5.3. The Model of the State's Protective Obligations in Horizontal Relations

5.3.1. Preliminary Remarks

The model of the state's protective obligations in horizontal relations is based on the assumption that the state safeguards constitutional rights, beholden to protect them against any violations, including those by private entities. The state's protective obligations cover the processes of both enacting and applying laws. Protection is provided through interference with potential or existing horizontal relations to the advantage of the weaker party and, at the

---

[288] As stated by S. Jarosz-Żukowska: 'Human rights (...) need norms of a private law as a kind of "key" to access private-legal relations, being objective guidelines of a system of values, impulses or factors radiating into the private law.' Cf. S. Jarosz-Żukowska, "Problem horyzontalnego stosowania...," p. 183.

same time, to the disadvantage of the stronger one. Thus the state's protective obligations are inevitably confronted with the autonomy of private entities. We should observe that individuals, both the weaker and the stronger ones, have very diverse expectations as to the scope of the state's protective obligations. On the one hand, individuals expect the state to respect their autonomy, decision-making freedom, or freedom of contract. They want the state not to interfere with the choice of the counterparty, with determining the contents of the contract and with its subsequent performance. On the other hand, when the contract they entered into turns out to be detrimental and unfair, and the other party skilfully exploits it, the weaker individuals do expect the state to act, to interfere with the contractual relation, to provide protection and assistance.[289]

Development of the conception of protective obligations of the state stems from the fact that currently individual's rights are infringed by private entities much more often than by the state. At least three reasons for this can be named. Firstly, there emerge more and more powerful private entities, such as international corporations, supranational non-governmental organizations, or global regulatory bodies, whose ability to subjugate an individual, including restraining his rights and freedoms, is similar to that of the state.[290] Secondly, the pursuit of business operators to maximize profits and promote their own interests, typical of free market economy, often takes place at the expense of consumers or employees, and thus involves infringements of their rights or freedoms. Thirdly, the more and more ubiquitous privatization of public tasks, which affects such areas of life as healthcare, education, energy supply or prison service, means that the degree of protection of rights and freedoms of the persons for whose benefit these tasks are performed is weakened.[291] Due to all these factors, currently it is not the actions of public authority, but those of private entities, that constitute the basic threat to individual's rights.

For this reason, contemporary democratic state shifted its position from a violator of rights of an individual to their guarantor, while the above new sources of threats make it necessary to extend the scope of the state's obligations and responsibilities. These responsibilities go beyond the traditional vertical relations and enter precisely the sphere of horizontal ones. This begs the question about the extent to which the state should protect an individual

---

[289] W. Osiatyński, *Prawa człowieka i ich granice...*, p. 309.

[290] *Cf.* A. Clapham, *Human Rights in the Private Sphere*, Oxford 2002, p. 137–138; Z. Kędzia, "Horyzontalne działanie praw...," p. 522–523.

[291] A. Barak, *Proportionality. Constitutional Rights...*, Cambridge 2012, p. 425.

from adverse effects of his own actions or unfavourable actions of private entities, including those able to unilaterally shape the individual's actual position. Undoubtedly, the limits of state interference with horizontal relations must be set in such a way to meet both the requirement of respecting individual's rights and that of protecting them. In other words, an individual must be given autonomy, the power to decide about himself, but at the same time efficient protection of his rights must be guaranteed.

5.3.2. Characteristics of the Model Based on Example of State Where it is Applied

The model of positive state obligations in the sphere of fundamental rights was formulated in the case law of the Federal Constitutional Court in mid 1970s and since then has been developed in Germany along with the model of the indirect horizontal effect of fundamental rights. The basic view underpinning both these models was that of the changing functions and tasks of the state via-a-vis the individual and the society.[292] This view embraced the shift in the state's position from that of the main potential violator of the individual's rights to that of their guarantor. The model of the indirect horizontal effect of constitutional rights puts greater emphasis on the requirement of implementation of these rights by courts, while the model of the state's positive obligations in the sphere of fundamental rights is more concerned with the legislator's tasks. In this sense these models complement each other. Individual's rights are protected by the legislator in a preventive manner, through private law norms, while by courts – in a repressive manner, through interpretation of indeterminate phrase and general clauses taking account of fundamental rights when resolving disputes between private entities.

The state's overall general obligation to protect the rights of the individual is derived from Art. 1 para. 1, second sentence, of the German Constitution, pursuant to which respecting and protecting human dignity is the duty of all state authority.[293] This concerns protection of dignity not so much against violations by the state, but rather against violations by private entities. Once

---

[292] Ch. Starck, "Human rights and private law in German constitutional development and in the judisdiction of the federal constitutional court" (in:) D. Friedmann, D. Barak-Erez, *Human Rights in Private Law*, Oxford 2002, p. 101; G. Dürig (in:) T. Maunz and others, *Grundgesetz...*, p. 66.

[293] Ch. Starck, "Human rights and private law...," p. 103; T. Langer, *Die Problematik der Geltung...*, p. 89.

the protective obligation covers human dignity, it also extends to subjective rights that stem from the said dignity. More detailed protective duties are inferred from the contents of constitutional provisions which enshrine individual fundamental rights.[294]

The doctrine of positive state obligations in the area of fundamental rights protection was formulated by the Federal Constitutional Court against the background of cases concerning hazards to human life or health resulting from actions of private entities.[295] It was subsequently developed in cases on contractual relations between private entities.[296] The common element in judgments issued in all these cases was the belief that basic rights express certain values the state has a duty to protect. Protection guaranteed by the state should be efficient, but it does not have an absolute character and extends only to the limits of foreseeability of a given hazard determined by the current state of science and technology.[297] It is the state authorities that decide how the protective duty is to be implemented, and they are also accountable for their decisions. The Federal Constitutional Court assumes that its intervention is possible only when courts commit an obvious infringement of the determination about the essence of the said right, embodied in the basic right.[298]

The conception of the state's protective duties in the sphere of horizontal relations, by its nature, is in a certain conflict with the conception of private autonomy, which assumes that parties to a contract are free to shape the legal relations between them and are responsible for the results. However, private autonomy exists only within the limits of applicable statutes, which in turn have to respect the basic constitutional rights. In principle, the state has to respect that autonomy; it can intervene only when one party to the contract has such a noticeable advantage over the other that it can actually impose certain contractual provisions. Then the aim of state interference is to restore

---

[294] T. Langer, *Die Problematik der Geltung...*, p. 91; Ch. Starck, "Human rights and private law...," p. 102.

[295] *Cf.* judgments of the Federal Constitutional Court: of February 25, 1975, Ref. No. 1 BvF 1, 2, 3, 4, 5, 6/74, BVerGE 39, 1 (*Schwangerschaftsabbruch I*); of October 16, 1977, Ref. No. 1 BvQ 5/77, BVerfGE 46, 160 (*Schleyer*); of August 8, 1978, Ref. No. 2 BvL 8/77, BVerfGE 49, 89 (*Kalkar I*); of January 14, 1981, Ref. No. 1 BvR 612/72, BVerfGE 56, 54 (*Fluglärm*); of May 28, 1993, Ref. No. 2 BvF 2/90 and 4, 5/92, BVerfGE 88, 203 (*Schwangerschaftsabbruch II*).

[296] *Cf.* judgments of the Federal Constitutional Court: of February 7, 1990, Ref. No. 1 BvR 26/84, BVerfGE 81, 242 (*Handelsvertreter*); of October 19, 1993, Ref. No. 1 BvR 567, 1044/89 BVerfGE 89, 214 (*Bürgschatfsvertäge*).

[297] Judgment of the Federal Constitutional Court of August 8, 1978, Ref. No. 2 BvL 8/77, BVerfGE 49, 89 (*Kalkar I*).

[298] Judgment of the Federal Constitutional Court of February 7, 1990, Ref. No. 1 BvR 26/84, BVerfGE 81, 242 (*Handelsvertreter*).

the upset balance of power, so as to accord the weaker party protection of his basic rights. The Federal Constitutional Court stresses that the state should not always interfere with contractual relations where there is no ideal balance between parties. It is only when 'structural subordination' of one party is found, for which party the contract's results are extremely disadvantageous, that legal opportunities to rectify such a contract should be provided.[299] Regulations in the field of the civil law that enable restoring the upset balance between parties include general clauses contained e.g. in § 138 para. 2 or § 242 of the German Civil Code.

5.3.3. The State as an Entity Beholden to Implement Constitutional Rights and Freedoms

The entities beholden to implement constitutional rights and freedoms are in principle public authorities.[300] However, the degrees of concretization of duties of public authorities in constitutional provisions vary.

Firstly, some constitutional provisions directly impose obligations on public authorities. And so according to Art. 30 of the Polish Constitution 'respect and protection [of human dignity] shall be the obligation of public authorities.'[301] Moreover, Art. 68 paras. 3 and 4 of the Constitution provide that 'Public authorities shall ensure special health care to children, pregnant women, handicapped people and persons of advanced age' and 'to combat epidemic illnesses and prevent the negative health consequences of degradation of the environment.' In this group of constitutional provisions we should also include those pursuant to which public authorities implement a specific task, despite lack of indication that implementation of this task is their duty. Provisions of this kind contain the so-called program norms, also called principles of the state's policy, and are particularly numerous in the subchapter of Chapter II entitled 'Economic, Social and Cultural Freedoms and Rights.' Those program norms, which have been mentioned earlier, sometimes only indicate socio-economic goals whose attainment is the obligation of public authorities, while in other cases identify the specific means which serve to

---

[299] Judgment of the Federal Constitutional Court of October 19, 1993, Ref. No. 1 BvR 567, 1044/89 BVerfGE 89, 214 (*Bürgschatfsvertäge*).

[300] Decision of the Polish Constitutional Tribunal of February 23, 2005, Ref. No. Ts 35/04.

[301] *Cf.* judgments of the Constitutional Tribunal: of April 11, 2001, Ref. No. K 11/00; of October 30, 2006, Ref. No. P 10/06; of July 9, 2009, Ref. No. SK 48/05; of February 24, 2010, Ref. No. K 6/09.

attain these goals.[302] An example of the latter kind of program norm is Art. 65 para. 5 of the Constitution, pursuant to which 'Public authorities shall pursue policies aiming at full, productive employment by implementing programmes to combat unemployment, including the organization of and support for occupational advice and training, as well as public works and economic intervention.' This provision lists examples of measures which serve to attain the desired goals, as demonstrated by the word 'including.' On the one hand, program norms of this kind oblige public authorities to undertake measures identified in their contents, serving to attain the desired goals, while on the other hand, they leave them freedom in choosing other measures useful in attaining the same goals. There are no doubts that program norms beget duties of public authorities, but there may be doubts about whether the same program norms beget any rights and freedoms of an individual, correlated with the said duties. The group of constitutional provisions which directly impose duties on public authorities should also include those which contain references to statutory regulation of a given right or freedom. What follows from such provisions is a duty to enact a statute, which is also an obligation of public authorities.

Secondly, some constitutional provisions formulate the state's obligations in a general manner, without concretizing their contents. The most frequent expression used in this context is that the 'Republic of Poland shall ensure' a certain freedom or protection of a specific good, for instance: 'The Republic of Poland shall (…) ensure the freedoms and rights of persons and citizens, the security of the citizens (…) and shall ensure the protection of the natural environment' (Art. 5 of the Constitution), 'The Republic of Poland shall ensure freedom for the creation and functioning of political parties' (Art. 11 of the Constitution), 'The Republic of Poland shall ensure freedom of the press and other means of social communication' (Art. 14 of the Constitution). The obligation to ensure a certain freedom or create conditions for the realization of a freedom or right each time requires a statutory concretization. At the same time, these provisions leave the choice of measures to serve such 'ensuring' of a freedom or right to the discretion of public authorities, the more so that the phrase is indeterminate.

Thirdly, some constitutional provisions formulate prohibitions for public authorities, which prohibitions should be treated as obligations to refrain from certain activities which interfere with the sphere of constitutional

---

[302] M. Florczak-Wątor, "Możliwości kontrolowania przez Trybunał Konstytucyjny swobody ustawodawcy w zakresie realizacji norm programowych," *Przegląd Sejmowy*, 4 (2009), p. 111 et. seq.

rights and freedoms. And so, 'Public authorities shall not acquire, collect nor make accessible information on citizens other than that which is necessary in a democratic state ruled by law' (Art. 51 para. 2). A similar interpretation should be used for Art. 53 para. 7, pursuant to which 'No one may be compelled by organs of public authority to disclose his philosophy of life, religious convictions or belief.'

Fourthly, some constitutional provisions confer a specific right on individuals with an indication that implementation of this right is the responsibility of public authorities. Examples of this kind of provisions may be Art. 32 para. 1 of the Constitution, which reads 'All persons shall have the right to equal treatment by public authorities,' or Art. 36 of the Constitution, pursuant to which 'A Polish citizen shall, during a stay abroad, have the right to protection by the Polish State.' Hence these are also examples of provisions which point at public authorities as the entity beholden to ensure implementation of a given right.

5.3.4. Positive Character of the State's Obligation to Protect Constitutional Rights and Freedoms of Individuals

It is beyond doubt that public authorities have negative obligations, which consist in the need to refrain from interfering with the sphere of constitutionally protected rights and freedoms of an individual. Many of the constitutional provisions quoted above indeed describe the state's obligations in these terms, by formulating prohibitions for public authorities. Yet, in those cases when private entities are prohibited from infringing constitutional rights and freedoms, the state's protective obligations have a positive character. The state becomes a watchdog of the observance of these prohibitions by private entities and at the same time their enforcement agency. This applies to prohibitions which may be infringed in horizontal relations, that is, the ban on scientific experiments, including medical ones, without voluntary consent of the person subjected to such experiments (Art. 39), ban on the use of torture and cruel, inhuman or degrading treatment (Art. 40), ban on compelling people to participate or not participate in religious practices (Art. 53 para. 6) or ban on permanent employment of children up to 16 years of age (Art. 65 para. 3).

Yet, an analysis of constitutional provisions leads to the conclusion that these are not the only positive obligations of public authority in a situation when constitutional rights and freedoms are infringed by private entities. The remaining positive obligations may be divided into two groups. The first one includes obligations which consist in safeguarding the protection of constitutional rights and freedoms from interference of other entities, including private ones. The other group should include obligations to create conditions for the implementation of constitutional rights and freedoms. Obligations from the first group are particularly important from the point of view of the problem of the horizontal effect of constitutional rights. They are not homogenous, however.

Some provisions of the Polish Constitution establish 'legal protection', that is, protection implemented under relevant legal regulations. Norms of this kind are found in Art. 31 para. 1 ('Freedom of the person shall receive legal protection'), Art. 38 ('The Republic of Poland shall ensure the legal protection of the life of every human being'), and Art. 47 ('Everyone shall have the right to legal protection of his private and family life, of his honor and good reputation'). In this case public authorities have the duty to enact specific legal regulations aimed at the protection of freedom, property and privacy. A more general obligation of 'legal protection' results from Art. 31 para. 3 of the Constitution. This provision allows the legislator to introduce restrictions upon the enjoyment of constitutional rights and freedoms of some persons 'to protect (…) freedoms and rights of other persons.'[303] Although this provision does not mention legal protection, is concerns precisely the protection guaranteed by statutes, because it is statutes that restrict the rights and freedoms of some persons in order to protect those of other persons.

The majority of constitutional provisions in which positive protective obligations are formulated do not, however, determine the way in they are to be discharged. Provisions of this sort may be divided into three groups. The first one covers provisions which refer the obligation of protection of a specific good, but without describing more specifically the obligation as such. Examples of provisions from this group include Art. 21 ('The Republic of Poland shall protect ownership and the right of succession') and Art. 24 ('Work shall be protected by the Republic of Poland'). The second group is made up of provisions establishing the right to protection of a specific good, such as Art. 68 para. 1 ('Everyone shall have the right to have his health protected') and Art. 72 para. 1 ('Everyone shall have the right to demand of organs of public authority that they defend children against violence, cruelty, exploitation and actions which undermine their moral sense'). Unlike the earlier group of provisions, the latter group emphasizes the subjective aspect (right to protection), and not the objective aspect, that is, the good which receives protection. The third group in-

---

[303] This condition was repeated in detailed limitation clauses contained in Art. 53 para. 5 and Art. 61 para. 3 of the Constitution.

cludes provisions which establish protection of rights of specific persons, such as protection of tenants' rights (Art. 75 para. 2), protection of rights resulting from discharge of parliamentary mandate (Art. 106), protection of consumers, customers, hirers or lessees (Art. 76). These provisions highlight the holders too, but unlike the first group, instead of referring to the right to protection, they mention the protection of all rights of persons of a specific kind.

Last, but not least, we can also find the state's protective obligations in those constitutional provisions which declare that the state will 'ensure' specific rights and freedoms. This concerns the provisions pursuant to which the 'Republic of Poland shall ensure': 'the freedoms and rights of persons and citizens, the security of the citizen' (Art. 5), 'the freedom for the creation and functioning of political parties' (Art. 11), or 'the freedom of the press and other means of social communication' (Art. 14). In the same group of provisions we should include Art. 68 para. 2 ('Equal access to health care services, financed from public funds, shall be ensured by public authorities to citizens, irrespective of their material situation') and Art. 70 para. 4 ('Public authorities shall ensure universal and equal access to education for citizens'). Ensuring the possibility to exercise a particular freedom or to access certain goods means not only an instruction to refrain from interfering with such freedom or from making access to such goods difficult, but also to remove obstacles which private entities create in this regard.

Although the provisions quoted above do not expressly name the source of threats to constitutional rights and freedoms, we should consider that they are concerned with actions and omissions of non-state entities. The state's positive protective obligations do not concern protection against actions of public authorities, because a sufficient degree of such protection is guaranteed by the state discharging its negative obligation in the form of prohibition of interference with the individual's rights and freedoms. So when speaking of positive obligations, I mean the situations when the state interferes with horizontal relations in order to protect the constitutional rights and freedoms of one party to these relations against actions of the other party, which are harmful for the former party.

First and foremost, protective obligations are discharged by the legislator in the sphere of law-making. It is the legislator's task to balance the values underlying the colliding rights and values, and then to determine the scope of protection of each of them. The constitutional requirement of 'wrapping' constitutional rights with statutory provisions is at the same time the requirement of ensuring the deserved protection of that right. As Andrzej Mączyński submits, 'What corresponds to the obligation concretized by statute is the subjective right enjoyed by specific persons, namely the right to demand that public authorities provide them with protection. This right is based on a provision of the Constitution, which requires complementing statutory provisions, nevertheless this should not be an obstacle to including it in the category of "constitutional rights."[304]

The state's protective obligations are finally concretized in the sphere of horizontal relations in the process of applying the law. All in all, it is the judiciary that will decide the scope of protection of constitutional rights and freedoms. Balancing of the underlying values requires taking into account the facts of individual examined cases. Hence the scope of protection of these rights and freedoms, determined in an abstract way by the legislator, is finally always concretized by the court adjudicating in disputes among private entities.

The problems relating to the state's protective obligations in the sphere of constitutional rights were also the subject of many decisions of the Polish Constitutional Tribunal. It is, after all, the body which assesses whether the legislator has appropriately balanced the values underlying constitutional rights and, consequently, correctly determined the scope of their protection. Although the Tribunal does not review the sphere of application of law, in cases of this sort it also examines the courts' jurisprudence in which the state's protective obligations are concretized against the backdrop of facts of cases. By way of example, in order to illustrate the context in which the Constitutional Tribunal examines the problem of the state's protective obligations in horizontal relations, it is worthwhile to mention a few judgments.

In the judgment of January 18, 2006, Ref. No. K 21/05, concerning the enjoyment of freedom of assembly in view of threats posed to this freedom by private entities, the Constitutional Tribunal held: 'public authorities have the duty to provide protection to groups which organize demonstrations and participate in them, because it is the only way in which freedom of assembly can be guaranteed in reality (…). It is an obligation of public authority to create effective conditions for holding a notified assembly when the behavior of other participants of public life might pose a threat to enjoyment of the freedom of association. (…) Public authority has an obligation to protect everyone who exercises his rights in a lawful manner.'

In turn in the judgment of May 28, 1997, Ref. No. K 26/96, reviewing the constitutionality of provisions which permit abortion in case of difficult living conditions or difficult personal situation of the pregnant woman, the Constitutional Tribunal pointed out the character of the protective

---

[304] A. Mączyński, "Konstytucyjne podstawy ochrony konsumentów" (in:) P. Tuleja, M. Florczak-Wątor, P. Kubas (eds.), *Prawa człowieka – społeczeństwo obywatelskie – państwo demokratyczne. Księga jubileuszowa dedykowana Profesorowi Pawłowi Sarneckiemu*, Warszawa 2010, p. 98. Similar view was promoted by M. Safjan, "Efekt horyzontalny...," p. 301.

obligation and the scope of its implementation. Firstly, it held that the intensity of protection of human life may vary at different stages of life and in different circumstances, yet it always has to be sufficient from the point of view of the protected good. Secondly, the Tribunal indicated that 'The ordinary legislator has authority only to determine the possible exceptions when – due to the collision of goods being constitutional values, or of constitutional rights or freedoms – it is necessary to sacrifice one of the colliding goods. The legislator's consent for sacrificing one of the colliding goods, resulting from a collision of a constitutional good with another constitutional good, right or freedom, does not deprive the said good of the feature of protected constitutional good.' This manner in which the legislator resolves the collision of goods which are constitutional values, or of constitutional rights or freedoms, is reviewed by the Constitutional Tribunal.

The state's positive protective obligations were particularly accentuated with respect to the right of ownership. Art. 64 para. 2 of the Constitution provides that ownership, other property rights and the right of succession are protected on an equal basis for everyone. In the ruling of May 26, 2009, Ref. No. SK 32/07, the Constitutional Tribunal stated that in its view 'the only subjective right which might be, through extensive interpretation, inferred from Art. 21 para. 1 of the Constitution is the individual right of every citizen to expect the legislator to discharge the obligation to protect ownership.' Similarly, in the judgment of June 29, 2005, Ref. No. SK 34/04, the Tribunal held that Art. 21 para. 1 of the Constitution imposes on the state a 'special duty to protect the right of ownership.'

5.3.5. Obligation for the State to Protect the Weaker Party to the Horizontal Relation

Against the background of the above provisions establishing positive obligations of the state in the field of the constitutional protection of the rights and freedoms of an individual, special attention – from the point of view of problems relating to the horizontal effect of constitutional rights – should be paid to those provisions which enable the state to interfere in a private law relation in order to protect the weaker party. In the Constitution, a structure of this kind is used in provisions on consumer and employment relations in the broad sense.

The first is the case of Art. 76 of the Constitution, pursuant to which 'Public authorities shall protect consumers, customers, hirers or lessees against activities threatening their health, privacy and safety, as well as against dishonest market practices.' The Tribunal stressed on many occasions that this provision gives 'the right to interfere in civil law relations.'[305] Also legal scholars accept that Art. 76 of the Constitution protects persons listed in it against activities of entities that are their market partners and professionally supply goods or services. Hence, as A. Mączyński submits, 'Art. 76 of the Constitution legitimizes involvement of public authorities in the sphere of relations between "private" entities, including those shaped in a contract.'[306] At the same time, we can notice in the Constitutional Tribunal case law that the scope of application of this provision is extended to cover all civil law relations in which one party has an actual advantage. According to the Tribunal, 'Art. 76 of the Constitution cannot be understood just as a provision intended to ensure a certain standard of protection exclusively to those entities it mentions expressly, while the constitutional notion of "consumer" (just like "hirer" or "lessee") cannot be understood only in its civil law meaning (…). The constitutional legislator took for granted that the consumer was the weaker party of a legal relation and for this reason needed protection, specifically certain rights which would lead to – at least relative – levelling of the counterparties' positions. Rights of the consumer are matched by certain duties of the other party, i.e., the vendor or service provider. And jointly, these rights of one party and duties of the other, are to compensate for the consumer's incomplete ability to benefit from the principle of autonomy of wills of parties to the contract. The constitutional provision indicates that protective obligations of public authorities include the need to provide minimum statutory guarantees to all entities which – despite their relations being shaped according to the principle of autonomy of wills – have a weaker position vis-à-vis professional participants of the market game.'[307] The Constitutional Tribunal expressed this view even more clearly in the judgment of September 13, 2005, Ref. No. K 38/04, concerning the language in which agreements are written. It held then that Art. 76 of the Constitution 'is the grounds for indicating that protective obligations of public authorities include the need to provide specific minimum statutory guarantees to all entities – in particular natural persons – which, even though their relations are shaped with respect for the principle of autonomy of wills, are in a weaker position, mainly, though

---

[305] Judgments of the Constitutional Tribunal: of October 10, 2000, Ref. No. P 8/99; of April 21, 2004, Ref. No. K 33/03; of May 17, 2006, Ref. No. K 33/05; of March 17, 2008, Ref. No. K 32/05; of December 2, 2008; Ref. No. K 37/07.

[306] A. Mączyński, "Konstytucyjne podstawy ochrony…," p. 96–97.

[307] Similarly cf. judgments of the Constitutional Tribunal: of October 10, 2000, Ref. No. P 8/99; of April 21, 2004, Ref. No. K 33/03; of May 17, 2006, Ref. No. K 33/05; of March 17, 2008, Ref. No. K 32/05; of December 2, 2008; Ref. No. K 37/07.

not exclusively, in economic terms, in their relation with professional participants of the market game.' But in another judgment, the Tribunal ruled out the possibility of placing the state's protective obligations resulting from Art. 76 of the Constitution, on housing cooperatives.[308]

The thesis that the weaker party of a private law relation is accorded stronger constitutional protection by the state is also shared by some legal scholars. Ewa Łętowska points out that 'consumer protection does not mean (...) that the authorities favor consumers in a protectionist manner, but take actions to compensate for their lack of knowledge and experience, resulting from the mass character of production and trade in general. This does not involve a privilege, but making up for the lost opportunities, returning to the idea which underlies the assumptions of the freedom of contract, restoring to them the conditions for assessment of the market situation (...). Projects and instruments which serve consumer protection are not (...) aimed to "give" consumers anything extra, but (...) to restore equality of opportunities that are lost with the development of modern manufacturing, trade or marketing. This is why (...) "consumer protection" is (...) an instrument of fight for a truly free market; free for all its participants, whether active or passive.'[309]

In the Polish private law, we can identify many examples of statutory regulations, the aim of which is to balance the positions of parties which are, so to speak, unequal by their nature. This concerns especially consumer relations in the broad sense, in which on the one side there is a professional: the entrepreneur, and on the other side, a non-professional: the consumer. Regulations of a preventive nature impose on the entrepreneurs information duties, introduce restrictions concerning freedom of creating standard contracts or protect consumers who enter into contracts in conditions of increased risk (distance and off-premises sales). Similarly, provisions having the nature of guarantees are those which exclude the possibility of termination of a lease contract made for a specified period of time or provisions which restrict the possibility of arbitrary increase of rent in flats which used to be governed by the regime of regulated rent. Some of these regulations have been reviewed by the Constitutional Tribunal, which on the one hand, assessed the efficien-

---

[308] *Cf.* judgments of the Constitutional Tribunal: of April 20, 2005, Ref. No. K 42/2002; of September 13, 2011, Ref. No. K 8/09.

[309] E. Łętowska, *Prawo umów konsumenckich*, Warszawa 1999, p. 19. On the subject of problems relating to giving effect to judicial protection of consumers, *cf.* E. Łętowska, M. Jagielska, K. Lis, P. Mikłaszewicz, A. Wiewiórowska-Domagalska, "Implementation of consumer law in Poland," *European Review of Private Law*, 6 (2007), p. 885 et. seq.

cy of protective mechanisms, and on the other, the need for them and the degree of interference with the sphere of an individual's freedoms.[310]

In two judgments issued in cases concerning regulated rent, on January 12, 2000, Ref. No. P 11/98, and on October 10, 2000, Ref. No. P 8/99, the Tribunal also emphasized that ensuring a certain degree of protection for landlords' rights need not automatically mean reducing the degree of protection that tenants' rights deserve. Both the aforementioned property rights may be protected using different means and procedures. Yet in the second judgment, the Constitutional Tribunal stressed that obligations imposed on public authorities by Art. 76 of the Constitution 'may be discharged in various ways: directly, by actual measures taken by public authorities (...) or indirectly, by the adequate shaping of legal provisions.' It should be borne in mind that public authorities cannot shift the burden of discharging their obligations in full on private persons. These obligations cannot be discharged exclusively by means of statutory regulation of duties imposed upon one party of a private law relation towards the other party of that relation, without any participation of public authorities.

The second case in which the Constitution expressly permits the state to interfere in a horizontal relation in order to protect the weaker party are the provisions on employment relations. Also in this case – like in the case of Art. 76 of the Constitution – the interference is of a preventive character and is not connected with the actual infringement of the employee's rights by the employer, but with the possibility of such an infringement. Pursuant to Art. 24 of the Constitution 'The State shall exercise supervision over the conditions of work.' This systemic principle is concretized in the state power to set the minimum wage (Art. 65 para. 4) or maximum norms of working hours (Art. 66 para. 2). A similar role is played by the legislator's determination of the manner of implementing the right to safe and hygienic conditions of work and the corresponding employer duties (Art. 66 para. 1). All these regulations which limit the freedom of parties to an employment relation in the area of shaping its substance aim to protect the employee.

The Constitutional Tribunal believes that 'work, performed under an employment relation in the broad sense, pursuant to the principle expressed in Art. 24 of the Constitution, is protected by the state. This means, however,

---

[310] Among examples of judgments concerning the issue of constitutionality of provisions shaping horizontal relations we can mention the Constitutional Tribunal judgments of: January 31, 2001, Ref. No. P 4/99 (succession of farms), April 28, 2003, Ref. No. K 18/02 (establishing paternity upon request of biological father), April 21, 2004, Ref. No. K 33/03 (bio-fuels), January 26, 2005, Ref. No. P 10/04 (bank writ of enforcement) or September 13, 2005, Ref. No. K 38/04 (language in which a contract is written).

that the state has an obligation to protect employees as the 'weaker' party of the employment relation. So what follows from the principle expressed in Art. 24 of the Constitution is the duty for the state to create guarantees of employee protection, including protection against unlawful or unjustified actions of employers. Neither from this principle and other constitutional provisions on work protection, nor from labor law provisions can it be inferred that the establishment of employment relations and the employer's actions under the said relations are a form of activity of public authorities. The actions taken by employers within the framework of employment relations, including termination of contracts or their termination with amendment of terms of pay and work, do not constitute an exercise of functions of public authority, so employers cannot be seen as a public authority within the meaning of Art. 77 para. 1 of the Constitution.'[311]

Authorizing the legislator to determine the scope of protection of a given right does not mean it can regulate completely freely or, the more so, in an arbitrary manner. What follows from the Constitution is a certain minimum protection determined by the essence of the given right or freedom.[312] The legislator cannot relinquish enacting the relevant protective instruments, likewise it cannot guarantee protection which is below the minimum standards determined by the constitutional regulation with respect to a given right. In this context, the protection would become an illusion.

5.3.6. Closing Remarks

The Polish Constitution in many various ways expresses the idea of protection of the individual by the state, yet in this context it does not apply so much to protecting the individual from actions of the state, but to protecting him against actions of private entities. The state is obliged to respect the rights of individuals and this is a sufficient guarantee of their protection in vertical relations. Hence the state's positive protective obligations do not concern the ban on interfering with the individual's rights, but, quite the contrary, the requirement to interfere in order to protect constitutional rights when they are infringed.

---

[311] Judgments of the Constitutional Tribunal: of October 18, 2005, Ref. No. SK 48/03; of October 24, 2006, Ref. No. SK 41/05; of July 12, 2011, Ref. No. K 26/09.

[312] J. Trzciński, "Naruszenie konstytucyjnych wolności lub praw jako podstawa skargi konstytucyjnej" (in:) *Zgromadzenie Ogólne Sędziów Trybunału Konstytucyjnego 10 marca 1999 roku, Studia i Materiały*, t. IX, Warszawa 1999, p. 45; A. Mączyński, "Konstytucyjne podstawy ochrony...," p. 99.

The matter of crucial importance is thus to determine what the state's obligations are in the light of the constitutional provisions.[313] On the one hand, the state has a duty not to infringe the individual's rights and not to interfere with their exercise, on the other hand it is required to create conditions for exercising such rights when this is necessary. Both obligations concern vertical relations. It is only the concept of the state's positive obligations in the sphere of protecting the individual's rights that extends the state's protective activity to cover horizontal relations. Not only is the state required to react when the rights of an individual are infringed by a private entity, but it also has the obligation to prevent such infringements. The latter aim is served by statutory provisions of preventive character, which for instance oblige the entrepreneur to provide consumers with reliable information about their rights, exclude the application of certain standard contracts or grant additional rights to consumers who enter into contracts under conditions of special risk (distance and off-premises sales). A similar type of guarantee is exhibited by provisions which exclude the possibility of terminating lease agreements made for a specified period of time or provisions restricting the possibility of arbitrary increases of rent in flats which once were governed by the regime of regulated rent. But the possibilities of restricting the rights and freedoms of individuals 'for their own good' in a preventive manner are limited. The impassable border of implementing the protective function is undoubtedly the need to respect the dignity of other beneficiaries of constitutional rights and freedoms, who also have the right to protection guaranteed by the Constitution. Thus implementation by the state of positive protective obligations requires balancing the values underlying the colliding rights and freedoms. The protection of constitutional rights of one private entity cannot deprive other private entities of the possibility to exercise – even if only to a certain extent – their, also guaranteed, constitutional rights.

---

[313] *Cf.* A. Barak, *Proportionality. Constitutional Rights...*, p. 422; M. Klatt, M. Meister, *The Constitutional Structure of Proportionality...*, p. 86.

CONCLUSION

The opening thesis for this monograph was the assertion that horizontal relations may not disregard those rights and freedoms which the Constitution guarantees to their parties. The constitutional provisions in this field have a restrictive impact both upon norms of private law, which must have regard for constitutional norms relating to rights and freedoms of an individual, as well as decisions by private entities that should shape their mutual relations with due regard for those rights. Thus, constitutional rights set the limits for the freedom of contract, or, more generally speaking, the autonomy of will of private entities. Endowing constitutional rights with a horizontal, and thereby also a universal, dimension is a necessary condition for ensuring their real protection. In a contemporary democratic country, it is usually not the functioning of state authorities, but that of private entities that poses the greatest threat to constitutional rights and freedoms. Some of these entities exercise powers comparable to state powers, and thus have a state-like capacity to subjugate individuals. Doubts as to whether these entities and their functioning fall under the private law or the public law trigger further doubts as to the nature of legal relations they engage in. It is so, since these relations are less and less traditional horizontal relations between equal entities, and more and more vertical relations resembling those existing between an individual and the state.

The main purpose of my research was to answer the question of how and to what extent constitutional rights can apply in horizontal relations under the Polish Constitution. Determining the effect of these rights was preceded by analyzing constitutional provisions, judicature and jurisprudence in selected countries, where this problem has enjoyed enduring popularity for decades now. This analysis allowed distinguishing three models of the horizontal effect of constitutional rights. These models are neither mutually exclusive nor do they compete with one another, hence their concordant application is possible and even desirable. Each of these models views the effect of constitutional rights in horizontal relations from a different perspective, and all of them pursue the same goal, namely guaranteeing an effective protection to an individual at all possible planes of his activity.

The model of the direct horizontal effect of constitutional rights is a subsidiary kind of model, which must be applied when there are no other options of protecting constitutional rights in horizontal relations. Under this model, the individual directly relies on the constitutional rights in relations with another entity because at the level of statutory law the protection of these rights is not guaranteed. This model of the horizontal effect can be applied only in the case of those rights and freedoms which are sufficiently clearly and precisely stipulated in the constitutional provisions, so that they can be autonomously applied. It should be added that, in this model, the individual cannot independently enforce his constitutional rights in his relations with another individual. Therefore, disputes against the background of these relations will need to ultimately be adjudicated by a court.

The model of the indirect horizontal effect of constitutional rights also implies the need to have regard for the substance of those rights by a court that adjudicates in a dispute between private entities; yet in this case the legal grounds for the claims by the party that brought the claim before the court is a statutory, rather than a constitutional, provision. Statutory provisions containing general clauses and indeterminate phrases are of fundamental importance for the adjudication in such a dispute. These statutory open concepts turn into some kind of gates, through which the values underlying constitutional rights are transposed into the private law, thus determining its interpretation and application.

Yet another model, which I call the model of protective obligations, accentuates even more the need for state activity in the field of protecting constitutional rights of the weaker party of horizontal relations against actions by the stronger party. Such protection must first be guaranteed by the legislator by way of creating private law norms that have regard for constitutional rights of both the parties to horizontal relations, and then by a court that adjudicates in a dispute relating to these norms. In both the cases, the state acts as a guarantor of constitutional rights, assuming the duty of protecting these rights against threats coming from private entities. It is worthy of note, as repeatedly emphasized in this book, that the boundaries between different models of applying constitutional rights is not clear. These models are mutually complementary and make certain common assumptions. Hence, legal scholars point out that the application of each of those models can give exactly the same effect.[314]

The problem of guaranteeing protection of constitutional rights in horizontal relations lies not only in construing an appropriate model of these

---

[314] *Cf.* M. Kumm, V. Ferreres Comella, "What is so special...," p. 246–247; Z. Kędzia, *Burżuazyjna koncepcja praw...*, p. 287; A. Łabno-Jabłońska, "Zasada bezpośredniego obowiązywania...," p. 78; B. Skwara, "Horyzontalny skutek praw...," p. 380–381.

relations being influenced by these rights, but also in setting the necessary limits of these rights. It must be kept in mind that, in horizontal relations, both the parties are the beneficiaries of constitutional rights and both may demand that these rights be protected. This makes the collision of constitutional rights in horizontal relations inevitable. Its resolution requires, in each and every case, the application of the mechanism of balancing values underlying constitutional rights. This mechanism is first used by the legislator to determine, in an abstract manner, the relation of precedence between colliding constitutional rights, then by a court which, based on these tenets and referring once again to constitutional axiology, adjudicates on collisions of these rights in a particular case. The mechanism of resolving collisions of constitutional rights is a necessary element of each and every model of their horizontal application, although it does reveal certain differences within the frame of individual models, which have been signaled in this book.

The models of the horizontal application of constitutional rights are the product of judicial decisions, hence the involvement of courts in protecting those rights is the condition for their application. Regard for the horizontal dimension of constitutional rights requires of the court to go beyond the text of a statute, which the court relies on in its adjudication, and to probe into constitutional values underlying these rights. This is a particularly challenging task for courts under the continental system of law, since these courts often tend to limit themselves to the literal interpretation of statutory provisions while adjudicating on the basis of a text of a statute. Hence, in the countries with a continental legal system, constitutional courts have played an immensely important role in a new way of looking at the essence of constitutional rights and, through their case law, these courts have initiated the practice of applying constitutional provisions that enshrine these rights. The ultimate success of the conception of the horizontal effect of constitutional rights is, however, the result of involving judges from other courts in a joint task of building a new idea of constitutionalism.[315] Greater awareness of the need to have regard for constitutional rights when adjudicating in disputes between private entities in Polish courts is also noticeable. This optimistic view is presented by not only Polish, but also foreign legal scholars. According to the Czech scholar Zdeněk Kühn, courts in Poland, juxtaposed against the background of courts in other countries of Central Europe, seem to be 'the most open to New Constitutionalism and a new constitutional

---

[315] Z. Kühn, "Making constitutionalism horizontal: Three different Central European strategies" (in:) A. Sajo, E. Uitz (eds.), *The Constitution in Private Relation. Expanding Constitutionalizm*, Ultrecht 2005, p. 226.

ideology of judicial decision-making, and it is they that have truly implement-ed the horizontal effect of basic rights in practice.'[316] The legitimacy of this thesis is confirmed by once notorious dispute between the Supreme Court and Supreme Administrative Court versus the Constitutional Tribunal on the courts' right to omit, in the process of adjudicating, of those statutes that are considered unconstitutional in the course of incidental review. The courts derived this right straight from the principle of the direct application of the Constitution, invoking the need to protect individuals' rights. The problem was, therefore, not that the courts were reluctant to refer to the Constitution, but that they did so in an excessive and possessive manner, transgressing the limits of powers reserved for the Constitutional Tribunal.[317]

Under the Polish Constitution, there is thus ample room to apply the above-described horizontal models of the application of constitutional rights. There are also favorable conditions for doing so created by the acceptance, in judicial decisions, of the need of the direct application of constitutional provisions. It also seems that we can venture a thesis on a growth of constitu-tional awareness of the Polish society, which is the result of not only an active judicial decision-making in the Constitutional Court, but also the presence of constitutional problems in the public debate and court litigation. However, the Polish jurisprudence has only just begun a substantive discussion on the problem of the method and scope of horizontal application of constitutional rights.

---

[316] Ibidem, p. 227.

[317] According to Z. Kühn, in Poland the said activism of judges in higher courts stems from the fact that a certain group of those judges, like the Constitutional Tribunal judges, have not followed a typical judicial career path, but were appointed as judges of the Supreme Court or the Supreme Administrative Court as law professors or representatives of jurisprudence. *Cf.* Z. Kühn, "Making constitutionalism…," p. 238–239.

BIBLIOGRAPHY

Abernathy G., "Expansion of the state action concept under the fourteenth amendment," *Cornell Law Quarterly*, 43 (1958).

Abramchayev L., "A social contract argument for the state's duty to protect from private violence," *St. John's Journal of Legal Commentary*, 18 (2004).

Aleinikoff T.A., "Constitutional law in the age of balancing," *The Yale Law Journal*, 96 (1987).

Alexy R., "Balancing, constitutional review, and representation," *International Journal of Constitutional Law*, 3 (2005).

Alexy R., "Constitutional rights, balancing, and rationality," *Ratio Juris*, 16 (2003).

Alexy R., "Discourse theory and fundamental rights" (in:) A.J. Menedez, E.O. Eriksen (eds.), *Arguing Fundamental Rights*, Dordrecht 2006.

Alexy R., "Postscript" (in:) R. Alexy, *A Theory of Constitutional Rights*, translation J. Rivers, Oxford 2002.

Alexy R., "Rights and liberties as concepts" (in:) M. Rosenfeld, A. Sajó (eds.), *The Oxford Handbook of Comparative Constitutional Law*, Oxford 2013.

Alexy R., *Theorie der Grundrechte*, Baden-Baden 1985.

Avbelj M., "Is there Drittwirkung in EU law?" (in:) A. Sajo, R. Uitz (eds.), *The Constitution in Private Relation: Expanding Constitutionalism*, Utrecht 2005.

Bałaban A., "Źródła prawa w polskiej konstytucji z 2 kwietnia 1997 r.," *Przegląd Sejmowy*, 5 (1997).

Balcarczyk J., *Prawo do wizerunku i jego komercjalizacja*, Warszawa 2009.

Balmer T.A., Thomas K., "In the balance: Thoughts on balancing and alternative approaches in state constitutional interpretation," *Albany Law Review*, 75 (2012–2013).

Banaszak B., "Ogólne wiadomości o prawach człowieka" (in:) B. Banaszak, A. Preisner, *Prawa i wolności obywatelskie w Konstytucji RP*, Warszawa 2002.

Banaszak B., "Prawa człowieka i obywatela w nowej Konstytucji Rzeczypospolitej Polskiej," *Przegląd Sejmowy*, 5 (1997).

Banaszak B., *Prawa jednostki i system ich ochrony*, Wrocław 1995.

Banaszak B., "Prezydencki projekty Karty praw i wolności," *Przegląd Sejmowy*, 1 (1993).

Banaszak B., *Sądownictwo konstytucyjne a ochrona podstawowych praw obywatelskich. RFN, Austria, Szwajcaria*, Wrocław 1990.

Banaszak B., "Skarga konstytucyjna i jej znaczenie w zakresie ochrony praw podstawowych" (in:) L. Wiśniewski (ed.), *Podstawowe prawa jednostki i ich sądowa ochrona*, Warszawa 1997.

Banaszak B., Preisner A., *Prawo konstytucyjne. Wprowadzenie*, Wrocław 1996.

Barak A., "Constitutional human rights and private law," *Review of Constitutional Studies*, 2 (1996).

Barak A., "Proportionality" (in:) M. Rosenfeld, A. Sajó (eds.), *The Oxford Handbook of Comparative Constitutional Law*, Oxford 2013.

Barak A., *Proportionality. Constitutional Rights and Their Limitations*, Cambridge 2012.

Barkhuysen T., Lindenbergh S.D. (eds.), *Constitutionalisation of Private Law*, Leiden 2006.

Bennett T.W., "Customary law and the drittwirkung of the South African Constitution" (in:) H. Scholler (ed.), *Gewohnheitsrecht und Menschenrechte. Aspekte eines vielschichtigen Beziehungssystems*, Baden-Baden 1998.

Bomhoff J., *Balancing Constitutional Rights. The Origins and Meanings of Postwar Legal Discourse*, Cambridge 2013.

Bomhoff J., "Balancing, the global and the local: Judicial balancing as a problematic topic in comparative (constitutional) law," *Hastings International and Comparative Law Review*, 31 (2008).

Bomhoff J., "Lüth's 50th anniversary: Some comparative observations on the german foundation of judicial balancing," *German Law Journal*, 9 (2008).

Bosek L., *Gwarancje godności ludzkiej i ich wpływ na polskie prawo cywilne*, Warszawa 2012.

Brinktrine R., "The horizontal effect of human rights in German constitutional law: The British debate on horizontality and the possible role model of the German doctrine of 'mittelbare Drittwirkung der Grundrechte'," *European Human Rights Law Review*, 4 (2001).

Brüggemeier G., "Constitutionalisation of private law – the German perspective" (in:) T. Barkhuysen, S.D. Lindenbergh (eds.), *Constitutionalisation of Private Law*, Leiden 2006.

Bryde Brun-Otto, "Fundamental rights as guidelines and inspirations: German constitutionalism in international perspective," *Wisconsin International Law Journal*, 25 (2007).

Butler A.S., "Constitutional rights in private litigation: a critique and comparative analysis," *Anglo-American Law Review*, 22 (1993).

Cali B., "Balancing human rights? Methodological problems with weights, scales and proportions," *Human Rights Quarterly*, 29 (2007).

Canaris C.W., *Grundrechte und Privatrechte*, Berlin–New York 1999.

Casey J., *Constitutional law in Ireland*, Dublin 2000.

Cheadle H., "Third party effect in the South African Constitution" (in:) A. Sajó, R. Uitz (eds.), *The Constitution in Private Relations. Expending Constitutionalism*, Utrecht 2005.

Cheadle H., Davis D., "The application of the 1996 Constitution in the private sphere," *South African Journal on Human Rights*, 13 (1997).

Cherednychenko O.O., "Fundamental rights and private law: A relationship of subordination or complementarity?," *Ultrecht Law Review*, 3 (2007).

Chmielarz A., *Funkcja prawna konstytucji na przykładzie Konstytucji Rzeczypospolitej Polskiej z 2 kwietnia 1997 roku*, Warszawa 2011.

Clapham A., *Human Rights in the Private Sphere*, Oxford 1993.

Clapham A., *Human Rights Obligations of Non-State Actors*, New York 2006.

Classen C. D., "Die Drittwirkung der Grundrechte in der Rechtsprechung des Bundesverfassungsgerichts," *Archiv des öffenlichen Rechts*, 122 (1997).

Cohen-Eliya M., Porat I., "Proportionality and the culture of justification," *The American Journal of Comparative Law*, 59 (2011).

Cohen-Eliya M., Porat I., "The hidden foreign law debate in Heller: The proportionality approach in American Constitutional Law," *San Diego Law Review*, 46 (2009).

Czarny P., Naleziński B., "Bezpośrednie stosowanie konstytucji; normy samowykonalne w konstytucji" (in:) J. Trzciński (ed.), *Charakter i struktura norm konstytucji*, Warszawa 1997.

Czarzasty J., "Przyczynek do problematyki klauzul generalnych," *Państwo i Prawo*, 5 (1978).

Drozd A., "Drittwirkung der Grundrechte im polnischen Recht mit besonderer Berücksichtigung des Arbeitsrechts," *Deutsche-Polnische Juristen-Zeitschrift*, 2008.

Du Bois F., "Private law in the age of rights" (in:) E. Reid, D. Visser (eds.), *Private Law and Human Rights. Bringing Rights Home in Scotland and South Africa*, Edinburgh 2013.

Du Bois F., "Rights trumped? Balancing in constitutional adjudication," *Acta Juridica*, 2004.

Dürig G., "Grundrechte und Zivilrechtsprechung" (in:) T. Maunz (ed.), *Von Bonner Grundgesetz zur gesamtdeutschen Verfassung. Festschrift zum 75. Geburtstag von Hans Nawiasky*, München 1956.

Dutkiewicz P., *Problem aksjologicznych podstaw prawa we współczesnej polskiej filozofii i teorii prawa*, Kraków 1996.

Działocha K., "Idea bezpośredniego stosowania konstytucyjnych wolności i praw" (in:) M. Jabłoński (ed.), *Wolności i prawa jednostki w Konstytucji RP*, Warszawa 2010.

Działocha K., "Stosowanie Konstytucji PRL," *Acta Universitatis Nicolai Copernici. Prawo XXIV*, 156 (1985).

Działocha K., "Zasada bezpośredniego stosowania konstytucji w dziedzinie wolności i praw obywateli" (in:) *Obywatel – jego wolności i prawa: zbiór studiów przygotowanych z okazji 10. lecia urzędu Rzecznika Praw Obywatelskich*, opr. B. Oliwa-Radzikowska, Warszawa 1998.

Egli P., *Drittwirkung von Grundrechten. Zugleich ein Beitrag zur Dogmatik der grundrechtlichen Schutzpflichten im Schweizer Recht*, Zurich 2002.

Ehrlich S. (ed.), *Teoria państwa i prawa*, Warszawa 1957.

Fastrich L., "Human rights and private law" (in:) K.S. Ziegler (ed.), *Human Rights and Private Law. Privacy as Autonomy*, Oregon 2007.

Faure M., van der Walt A. (eds.), *Globalization and Private Law. The Way Forward*, Cheltenham 2010.

Fedtke J., *Drittwirkung in Germany* (in:) D. Oliver, J. Fedtke (eds.), *Human Rights and the Private Sphere. A Comparative Study*, New York 2007.

Fedtke J., *South Africa. From indirect to direct effect in South Africa: A System in transition* (in:) D. Oliver, J. Fedtke (eds.), *Human Rights and the Private Sphere. A Comparative Study*, New York 2007.

Filipek J., "Jeszcze o sankcji prawnej," *Państwo i Prawo*, 4 (1965).

Florczak-Wątor M., *Horyzontalny wymiar praw konstytucyjnych*, Kraków 2014.

Florczak-Wątor M., "Kontrola konstytucyjności klauzul generalnych," *Przegląd Sejmowy*, 4 (2013).

Florczak-Wątor M., "Możliwość kontrolowania przez Trybunał Konstytucyjny swobody ustawodawcy w zakresie realizacji norm programowych," *Przegląd Sejmowy*, 4 (2009)

Florczak-Wątor M., "O potrzebie ustawowego uregulowania trybu rozpatrywania petycji," *Zeszyty Prawnicze BAS*, 2 (2013).

Florczak-Wątor, "Wątpliwości dotyczące wyjątku od zasady bezpośredniego stosowania Konstytucji RP" (in:) *Zagadnienia Sądownictwa Konstytucyjnego*, 2 (2012).

Forde M., *Constitutional Law*, Dublin 2004.

Garlicki L., "Aksjologiczne podstawy reinterpretacji konstytucji" (in:) M. Zubik (ed.), *Dwadzieścia lat transformacji ustrojowej w Polsce*, Warszawa 2010.

Garlicki L., "Bezpośrednie stosowanie konstytucji" (in:) *Konferencja naukowa: Konstytucja RP w praktyce (materiały z konferencji)*, Warszawa 1999.

Garlicki L. (ed.), *Konstytucja Rzeczypospolitej Polskiej. Komentarz*, Warszawa 2002, 2007.

Garlicki L., "Ochrona konstytucyjności i praworządności," *Państwo i Prawo*, 10 (1987).

Gizbert-Studnicki T., "O nieważnych czynnościach prawnych w świetle koncepcji czynności konwencjonalnych," *Państwo i Prawo*, 4 (1975).

Gizbert-Studnicki T., "Zasady i reguły prawne," *Państwo i Prawo*, 3 (1988).

Gizbert-Studnicki T., Grabowski A., "Normy programowe w konstytucji" (in:) J. Trzciński (ed.), *Charakter i struktura norm konstytucji*, Warszawa 1997.

Góralczyk-Papoń A., "Klauzule generalne w prawie cywilnym – zagrożenie dla porządku prawnego, czy instrument dostosowawczy prawa do zmiennych warunków gospodarczych?," *Humanistyczne Zeszyty Naukowe – Prawa Człowieka*, 7 (2000).

Górski J., "Aksjologiczne przesłanki decyzji sądowych w sprawach gospodarczych" (in:) K. Pałecki (ed.), *Dynamika wartości w prawie*, Kraków 1997.

Granat M., "W sprawie niektórych kwestii związanych z podpisywaniem przez kandydatów na posłów weksli in blanco," *Przegląd Sejmowy*, 2 (2007).

Greer P., "'Balancing' and the European Court of Human Rights: a Contribution to the Habermas – Alexy debate," *Cambridge Law Journal*, Vol. 63/2004.

Groszyk H., Leszczyński L., "Wartości pozaprawne w procesie stosowania klauzul generalnych" (in:) H. Rot (ed.), *Problemy metodologii i filozofii prawa*, Wrocław 1988.

Grzybowski S. (ed.), *System prawa cywilnego*, t. I, *Część ogólna*, Wrocław–Warszawa–Kraków–Gdańsk 1974.

Grzybowski S., "Struktura i treść przepisów prawa cywilnego odsyłających do zasad współżycia społecznego," *Studia Cywilistyczne*, VI (1965).

Guckelberger A., "Die Drittwirkung der Grundrechte," *Juristische Schulung*, 12 (2013).

Gutowski M., *Nieważność czynności prawnej*, Warszawa 2012.

Hauser R., "Zapytajcie Trybunał," *Rzeczpospolita*, March 18, 2002.

Höfling W., Burkiczak Ch., "Die unmittelbare Drittwirkung gemäß Art. 9 Abs. 3 Satz GG," *Recht der Arbeit*, 5 (2004).

Hunt M., "The 'Horizontal Effect' of the Human Rights Act," *Public Law*, 1998.

Jabłoński M., „Zakres podmiotowy realizacji praw obywatelskich w Konstytucji RP z 2.4.1997 r." (in:) B. Banaszak, A. Preisner (eds.), *Prawa i wolności obywatelskie w Konstytucji RP*, Warszawa 2002.

Jakimowicz W., *Publiczne prawa podmiotowe*, Kraków 2002.

Jamróz A., "Bezpośrednie stosowanie konstytucji w kontekście jej normatywnego charakteru. Kilka refleksji" (in:) I. Bogucka, Z. Tobor (eds), *Prawoznawstwo a praktyka stosowania prawa*, Katowice 2002.

Jamróz L., *Skarga konstytucyjna. Wstępne rozpoznanie*, Białystok 2011.

Jarosz-Żukowska S., "Problem horyzontalnego stosowania norm konstytucyjnych dotyczących wolności i praw jednostki w świetle Konstytucji RP" (in:) M. Jabłoński (ed.), *Wolności i prawa jednostki w Konstytucji RP*, Warszawa 2010.

Jastrzębski J., Zubik M., "Mandat wolny versus weksel," *Przegląd Sejmowy*, 2 (2007).

Kaczor J., "Z problematyki klauzul generalnych w Konstytucji RP" (in:) A. Bator (ed.), *Z zagadnień teorii i filozofii prawa. Konstytucja*, Wrocław 1999.

Kaźmierczyk S., "O bezpośrednim stosowaniu przepisów konstytucji" (in:) I. Bogucka, Z. Tabor (eds.), *Prawo a wartości. Księga jubileuszowa Profesora Józefa Nowackiego*, Kraków 2003.

Kaźmierczyk S., "Sankcja konstytucji jako zagadnienie metodologiczne" (in:) A. Bator (ed.), *Z zagadnień teorii i filozofii prawa. Konstytucja*, Wrocław 1999.

Kędzia Z., *Burżuazyjna koncepcja praw człowieka*, Wrocław–Warszawa–Kraków–Gdańsk 1980.

Kędzia Z., "Horyzontalne działanie praw obywatelskich" (in:) J. Łętowski (ed.), *Państwo, prawo, obywatel*, Wrocław–Warszawa–Kraków–Gdańsk–Łódź 1989.

Kędzia Z., "Uwagi o aksjologii konstytucji" (in:) A. Rzepliński (ed.), *Prawa człowieka w społeczeństwie obywatelskim*, Warszawa 1993.

Klatt M., Meister M., *The Constitutional Structure of Proportionality*, Oxford 2012.

Kolasiński K., "Zaskarżalność ustaw w drodze pytań prawnych do Trybunału *Konstytucyjnego*," *Państwo i Prawo*, 9 (2001).

Konferencja naukowa: Konstytucja RP w praktyce (materiały z konferencji), Warszawa 1999.

Kordela M., *Zarys typologii uzasadnień aksjologicznych w orzecznictwie Trybunału Konstytucyjnego*, Poznań 2001.

Kozak A., "Konstytucja jako podstawa decyzji stosowania prawa" (in:) A. Bator (ed.), *Z zagadnień teorii i filozofii prawa*, Wrocław 1999.

Kręcisz W., "Stanowisko sądów powszechnych wobec bezpośredniego stosowania Konstytucji," *Acta Universitatis Wratislaviensis, Przegląd Prawa Administracyjnego*, LX (2004).

Kühn Z., "Making constitutionalism horizontal: Three different Central European strategies" (in:) A. Sajo, E. Uitz (eds.), *The Constitution in Private Relation. Expanding Constitutionalizm*, Ultrecht 2005.

Kumm M., "Who is afraid of the total constitution? Constitutional rights as principle and the constitutionalization of private law," *German Law Journal*, 4 (2006).

Kumm M., Ferreres Comella V., "What is so special about constitutional rights in private litigation? A comparative analysis of the function of state action requirements and indirect horizontal effect" (in:) A. Sajo, R. Uitz (eds.), *The Constitution in Private Relations. Expanding Constitutionalism*, Utrecht 2005.

Kunicki A., "Art. 3 p.o.p.p. de lege ferenda," *Państwo i Prawo*, 9 (1960)

Laing S., Visser D., "Principles, policy and practice: Human rights and the law of contract" (in:) E. Reid, D. Visser (eds.), *Private Law and Human Rights. Bringing Rights Home in Scotland and South Africa*, Edinburgh 2013.

Lang Temple J., "Private law aspects of the Irish constitution," *Irish Jurist*, 6 (1971).

Langer T., *Die Problematik der Geltung der Grundrechte zwischen Privaten*, Frankfurt 1998.

Leisner W., *Grundrechte und Privatrecht*, München 1960.

Lenckner T., "The Principle of interest balancing as a general basis of justification," *Brigham Young University Law Review* 1986.

Leszczyński L., "Funkcje klauzul odsyłających a model ich tworzenia w systemie prawa," *Państwo i Prawo*, 7 (2000).

Leszczyński L., "Konstrukcje otwarte tekstu prawnego wobec zmian społecznych" (in:) H. Rot (ed.), *Prawo i prawoznawstwo wobec zmian społecznych*, Wrocław 1990.

Leszczyński L., "Praworządne stosowanie prawa a klauzule generalne," *Państwo i Prawo*, 11 (1989).

Leszczyński L., "Właściwości posługiwania się klauzulami generalnymi w prawie prywatnym. Perspektywa zmiany trendu," *Kwartalnik Prawa Prywatnego*, 3 (1995).

Lindenbergh S., "Fundamental rights in private law. Anchors or goals in a globalizing legal order?" (in:) M. Faure, A. van der Walt (eds.), *Globalization and Private Law. The Way Forward*, Cheltenham 2010.

Linders H., *Über der Frage der unmittelbaren Beteutung der Grundrechtsbestimmungen des Bonner Grundgesetzes für der privatrechtlichen Rechtsverkehr (Ein Beitrag zum Problem der „Drittwirkung" der Grundrechtsbestimmungen)*, Münster 1961.

Liszcz T., *Nieważność czynności prawnej w umownych stosunkach pracy*, Warszawa 1977.

Lücke J., "Die Drittwirkung der Grundrechte am Hand des Art. 19 Abs. 3 GG," *Juristenzeitung*, 54 (1999).

Łabno-Jabłońska A., "Zasada bezpośredniego obowiązywania konstytucyjnych praw i wolności jednostki. Analiza prawno porównawcza" (in:) L. Wiśniewski (ed.), *Podstawowe prawa jednostki i ich sądowa ochrona*, Warszawa 1997.

Łętowska E., "Bariery naszego myślenia o prawie w perspektywie integracji z Europą," *Państwo i Prawo*, 4–5 (1996).

Łętowska E., "Interpretacja a subsumpcja zwrotów niedookreślonych i nieostrych," *Państwo i Prawo*, 7–8 (2011).

Łętowska E., *Prawo umów konsumenckich*, Warszawa 1999.

Łętowska E., Jagielska M., Lis K., Mikłaszewicz P., Wiewiórowska-Domagalska A., "Implementation of consumer law in Poland," *European Review of Private Law*, 6 (2007).

Madry A.R., "State action and the obligation of the states to prevent private harm: the rehnquist transformation and the betrayal of fundamental commitments," *Southern California Law Review*, 65 (1992).

Marauhn T., Ruppel N., "Balancing conflicting human rights: Konrad Hesse's notion of 'Praktische Konkordanz' and the German Federal Constitutional Court" (in:) Brems E. (ed.), *Conflicts Between Fundamental Rights*, Antwerp 2008.

Masternak-Kubiak M., "Prawo do równego traktowania" (in:) B. Banaszak, A. Preisner (eds.), *Prawa i wolności obywatelskie w Konstytucji RP*, Warszawa 2002.

Maunz T., Dürig G., Herzog R., Scholz R., Lerche P., Papier H-J., Randelzhofer A., Schmidt-Assmann E., *Grundgesetz. Kommentar, Band I*, Munchen 1990.

Mączyński A., "Bezpośrednie stosowanie konstytucji przez sądy," *Państwo i Prawo*, 5 (2000).

Mączyński A., "Konstytucyjne podstawy ochrony konsumentów" (in:) P. Tuleja, M. Florczak-Wątor, S. Kubas (eds.), *Prawa człowieka – społeczeństwo obywatelskie – państwo demokratyczne. Księga jubileuszowa dedykowana Profesorowi Pawłowi Sarneckiemu*, Warszawa 2010.

Möller K., *The Global Model of Constitutional Rights*, Oxford 2012.

Nieuwenhuis H., "Fundamental rights talk. An enrichment of legal discourse in private law?" (in:) T. Barkhuysen, S. D. Lindenbergh (eds.), *Constitutionalisation of Private Law*, Leiden 2006.

Nipperdey H.C., "Gleicher Lohn der Frau für gleiche Leistung. Ein Beitrag zur Auslegung der Grundrechte," *Recht der Arbeit*, 1950.

Nita B., "Bezpośrednie stosowanie konstytucji a rola sądów w ochronie konstytucyjności prawa," *Państwo i Prawo*, 9 (2002).

Niżnik-Mucha A., "Kilka refleksji na temat wartości konstytucyjnych w świetle założeń pozytywizacji praw człowieka," *Przegląd Prawa Prywatnego*, 7–8 (2010).

Novak M., "Three models of balancing (in constitutional review)," *Ratio Juris*, 1 (2010).

Nowacki J., *Praworządność. Wybrane problemy teoretyczne*, Warszawa 1977.

Nowacki J., "Problem blankietowości przepisów zawierających klauzule generalne" (in:) G. Skąpska and others (eds.), *Prawo w zmieniającym się społeczeństwie. Księga Jubileuszowa Profesor Marii Boruckiej-Arctowej*, Kraków 1992.

O'Cinneide C., "Irish constitutional law and direct horizontal effect – a successful experiment?" (in:) D. Oliver, J. Fedtke (eds.), *Human Rights and the Private Sphere. A Comparative Study*, New York 2007.

Oeter S., "Fundamental rights and their impact on private law – doctrine and practice under the German Constitution," *Tel Aviv University Studies in Law*, 12 (1994).

Oliver D., Fedtke J., "Comparative analysis" (in:) D. Oliver, J. Fedtke (eds.), *Human Rights and the Private Sphere. A Comparative Study*, New York 2007.

Oliver D., Fedtke J. (eds.), *Human Rights and the Private Sphere. A Comparative Study*, New York 2007.

Osiatyński W., *Prawa człowieka i ich granice*, Kraków 2011.

Pałecki K., "Wstęp" (in:) K. Pałecki (ed.), *Dynamika wartości w prawie*, Kraków 1997.

Pałecki K., "Zmiany w aksjologicznych podstawach prawa jako wskaźnik jego tranzycji" (in:) K. Pałecki (ed.), *Dynamika wartości w prawie*, Kraków 1997.

Petersen N., "How to compare the length of lines to the weight of stones: Balancing and the resolution of value conflicts in constitutional law," *German Law Journal*, 14 (2013).

Piechowiak M., "Pojęcie praw człowieka" (in:) L. Wiśniewski (ed.), *Podstawowe prawa jednostki i ich sądowa ochrona*, Warszawa 1997.

Pietrzykowski K., "Glosa do wyroku SN z 11 marca 1997 r., sygn. III CKN 34/97," *OSP*, 10 (1997).

Preisner A., "Dookoła Wojtek. Jeszcze o bezpośrednim stosowaniu Konstytucji RP" (in:) L. Garlicki, A. Szmyt, *Sześć lat Konstytucji Rzeczypospolitej Polskiej. Doświadczenia i inspiracje*, Warszawa 2003.

Preuß U., "The German drittwirkung doctrine and its socio-political background" (in:) A. Sajo., R. Uitz (eds.), *The Constitution in Private Relations: Expanding Constitutionalism*, Utrecht 2005.

Preussner-Zamorska J., *Nieważność jako postać wadliwości czynności prawnej*, Kraków 1977.

Projekty Konstytucji 1993–1997, cz. I, edited for print by R. Chruściak, Warszawa 1997.

Projekty konstytucyjne 1989–1991, edited for print by M. Kallas, Warszawa 1992.

Radwański Z., *Teoria umów*, Warszawa 1977.

Radwański Z., Zieliński M., "Uwagi *de lege ferenda* o klauzulach generalnych w prawie prywatnym," *PLeg*, 2 (2001).

Redelbach A., Wronkowska S., Ziembiński Z., *Zarys teorii państwa i prawa*, Warszawa 1992.

Reid E., Visser D. (eds.), *Private Law and Human Rights. Bringing Rights Home in Scotland and South Africa*, Edinburgh 2013.

Reimers W., *Die Bedeutung der Grundrechte für das Privatrecht*, 1958.

Rösler H., "Harmonizing the German civil code of the nineteenth century with a modern constitution – the Lüth Revolution 50 years ago in comparative perspective," *Tulane European and Civil Law Forum*, 23 (2008).

Rott-Pietrzyk E., "Klauzule generalne rozsądku w kodeksie cywilnym," *Kwartalnik Prawa Prywatnego*, 3 (2005).

Sadurski W., "Konstytucja Muminków," *Rzeczpospolita*, June 10, 1996.

Safjan M., "Efekt horyzontalny praw podstawowych w prawie prywatnym: autonomia woli a zasada równego traktowania," *Kwartalnik Prawa Prywatnego*, 2 (2009).

Safjan M., "Klauzule generalne w prawie cywilnym (przyczynek do dyskusji)," *Państwo i Prawo*, 11 (1990).

Safjan M., "Refleksje wokół konstytucyjnych uwarunkowań rozwoju ochrony dóbr osobistych," *Kwartalnik Prawa Prywatnego*, 1 (2002).

Safjan M., "Zasada swobody umów (Uwagi wstępne na tle wykładni art. 353^1 k.c.)," *Państwo i Prawo*, 4 (1993).

Sajo A., Uitz R. (eds.) *The Constitution in Private Relations: Expanding Constitutionalism*, Utrecht 2005.

Sarnecki P., "Idee przewodnie Konstytucji Rzeczypospolitej Polskiej z 2 kwietnia 1997 r.," *Przegląd Sejmowy*, 5 (1997).

Sarnecki P., "Normy programowe w Konstytucji i odpowiadające im wolności obywatelskie" (in:) L. Garlicki, A. Szmyt (eds.), *Sześć lat Konstytucji Rzeczypospolitej Polskiej. Doświadczenia i inspiracje*, Warszawa 2003.

Sarnecki P., "Stosowanie Konstytucji PRL w orzecznictwie Naczelnego Sądu Administracyjnego," *Studia Prawnicze*, 3 (1988).

Scanlon T.M., "Adjusting rights and balancing values," *Fordham Law Review*, 72 (2004).

Schlink B., "Proportionality" (in:) M. Rosenfeld, A. Sajó (eds.), *The Oxford Handbook of Comparative Constitutional Law*, Oxford 2013.

Shaman J.M., *Constitutional Interpretation. Illusion and Reality*, Westport 2001.

Skwara B., "Horyzontalne obowiązywanie praw człowieka. Rozważania teoretycznoprawne" (in:) J. Jaskiernia (ed.), *Efektywność europejskiego systemu ochrony praw człowieka. Ewolucja i uwarunkowania systemu ochrony praw człowieka*, Toruń 2012.

Skwara B., "Horyzontalny skutek praw i wolności jednostki w systemie Konstytucji RP" (in:) T. Gardocka, J. Sobczak (eds.), *Dylematy praw człowieka*, Toruń 2008.

Skwara B., "Poziome obowiązywanie praw człowieka w świetle Konstytucji RP," *Homines Hominibus*, 1 (2009).

Słownik języka polskiego PWN, http://sjp.pwn.pl; P. Żmigrodzki (ed.), *Wielki słownik języka polskiego*, http://wsjp. pl.

Smits J., "Private law and fundamental rights: a sceptical view" (in:) T. Barkhuysen, S.D. Lindenbergh (eds.), *Constitutionalisation of Private Law*, Leiden 2006.

Sobolewski P., "Kontrowersje wokół pojęcia nieistnienia i nieważności czynności prawnej," *Przegląd Prawa Handlowego*, 5 (2009).

Starck Ch., "Human rights and private law in German constitutional development and in the judisdiction of the federal constitutional court" (in:) D. Friedmann, D. Barak-Erez, *Human Rights in Private Law*, Oxford 2002.

Stelmachowski A., "Klauzule generalne w kodeksie cywilnym (Zasady współżycia społecznego – społeczno-gospodarcze przeznaczenie prawa)," *Państwo i Prawo*, 1 (1965).

Stelmachowski A., "Znaczenie klauzuli generalnej zawartej w art. 386 k.c. w obrocie uspołecznionym," *Przegląd Ustawodawstwa Gospodarczego*, 6 (1968).

Stone Sweet A., Mathews J., "Proportionality balancing and global constitutionalism," *Columbia Journal of Transnational Law*, 47 (2008).

Szmulik B., *Skarga konstytucyjna na tle porównawczym*, Warszawa 2006.

Trzciński J., "Naruszenie konstytucyjnych wolności lub praw jako podstawa skargi konstytucyjnej" (in:) *Zgromadzenie Ogólne Sędziów Trybunału Konstytucyjnego 10 marca 1999 roku. Studia i materiały*, t. IX, Warszawa 1999.

Trzciński J., "Podmiotowy zakres skargi konstytucyjnej" (in:) L. Garlicki (ed.), *Konstytucja. Wybory. Parlament. Studia ofiarowane Zdzisławowi Jaroszowi*, Warszawa 2000.

Trzciński J., "Zakres podmiotowy i podstawa skargi konstytucyjnej" (in:) J. Trzciński (ed.), *Skarga konstytucyjna*, Warszawa 2000.

Tuleja P., *Normatywna treść praw jednostki w ustawach konstytucyjnych RP*, Warszawa 1997.

Tuleja P., "Stosowanie Konstytucji RP przez sądy" (in:) O. Bogucki, J. Ciapała, P. Mijal (eds.), *Standardy konstytucyjne a problem władzy sądowniczej i samorządu terytorialnego*, Szczecin 2008.

Tuleja P., *Stosowanie Konstytucji RP w świetle zasady jej nadrzędności (wybrane problemy)*, Kraków 2003.

Tushnet M., "An essay on rights," *Texas Law Review*, 8 (1984).

Voermans W., "Applicability of fundamental rights in private law: What is the legislature to do? An intermezzo from a constitutional point of view" (in:) T. Barkhuysen, S.D. Lindenbergh (eds.), *Constitutionalisation of Private Law*, Leiden 2006.

Vogt G., *Die Drittwirkung der Grundrechte und Grundrechtsbestimmungen des Bonner Grundgesetzes*, Münster 1960.

Waldziński S., "Stosowanie Konstytucji w orzecznictwie sądowym" (in:) D. Dudek, A. Janicka, W.S. Staszewski (eds.), *Ius et Veritas. Księga poświęcona pamięci Michała Staszewicza*, Lublin 2003.

Walt J. van der, "Progressive indirect horizontal application of the bill of rights: Towards a co-operative relation between common-law and constitutional jurisprudence," *South African Journal on Human Rights*, 17 (2001).

Wasilewski A., "Przedstawianie pytań prawnych Trybunałowi Konstytucyjnemu przez sądy (art. 193 Konstytucji)," *Państwo i Prawo*, 8 (1999).

Webber G.C.N., "Proportionality, balancing, and the cult of constitutional rights scholarship," *Canadian Journal of Law and Jurisprudence*, 1 (2010).

Winczorek P., *Dyskusje konstytucyjne*, Warszawa 1996.

Wiśniewski L., "Dla kogo konstytucja," *Rzeczpospolita*, October 9,1996.

Wiśniewski L., "Tor przeszkód projektu nowej konstytucji," *Rzeczpospolita*, June 20,1996.

Wójcik K., "Klauzule generalne a pojęcia prawne i prawnicze (zasady prawa i społeczne niebezpieczeństwo czynu)," *Studia Prawno-Ekonomiczne*, t. XLV (1990).

Wójcik K., "Klauzule generalne a zmiany społeczne" (in:) H. Rot (ed.), *Prawo i prawoznawstwo wobec zmian społecznych*, Wrocław 1990.

Wójcik K., "Teoretyczna konstrukcja klauzuli generalnej," *Studia Prawno-Ekonomiczne*, VLIV (1990).

Wojtyczek K., *Granice ingerencji ustawodawczej w sferę praw człowieka w Konstytucji RP*, Kraków 1999.

Wojtyczek K., "Horyzontalny wymiar praw człowieka zagwarantowanych w Konstytucji RP," *Kwartalnik Prawa Prywatnego*, 2 (1999).

Wojtyczek K., "Konstytucyjne regulacje systemu wyborczego w III Rzeczypospolitej" (in:) F. Rymarz (ed.), *10 lat demokratycznego prawa wyborczego Rzeczypospolitej Polskiej (1990–2000)*, Warszawa 2000.

Wojtyczek K., *Sądownictwo konstytucyjne w Polsce. Wybrane zagadnienia*, Warszawa 2013.

Wróblewski J., "Tworzenie prawa a wykładnia prawa," *Państwo i Prawo*, 6 (1978).

Wronkowska S., *Podstawowe pojęcia prawa i prawoznawstwa*, Poznań 2005.

Wronkowska S., "W sprawie bezpośredniego stosowania Konstytucji," *Państwo i Prawo*, 9 (2001).

Wronkowska S., Ziembiński Z., *Zarys teorii prawa*, Poznań 2001.

Wyrozumska A., "Direct application of the polish constitution and international treaties to private conduct," *Polish Yearbook of International Law*, 25 (2001).

Ziegler K. J. (ed.), *Human Rights and Private Law. Privacy as Autonomy*, Oregon 2007.

Zieliński T., "Klauzule generalne w demokratycznym państwie prawnym," *Studia Iuridica* XXIII (1992).

Zieliński T., *Klauzule generalne w prawie pracy*, Warszawa 1988.

Zieliński T., *Wykładnia prawa. Zasady, reguły, wskazówki*, Warszawa 2002.

Ziembiński Z., *Etyczne problemy prawoznawstwa*, Wrocław 1972.

Ziembiński Z., "Kilka uwag o pojęciu przestrzegania i pojęciu stosowania prawa," *Państwo i Prawo*, 1 (1968).

Ziembiński Z., *Normy moralne a normy prawne. Zarys problematyki*, Poznań 1963.

Ziembiński Z., "O normie prawnej" (in:) S. Wronkowska (ed.), *Z teorii i filozofii prawa Zygmunta Ziembińskiego*, Łódź 2007.

Ziembiński Z., "Stan dyskusji nad problematyką klauzul generalnych," *Państwo i Prawo*, 3 (1989).

Ziembiński Z., *Wartości konstytucyjne. Zarys problematyki*, Warszawa 1993.

Technical Editor
Anna Poinc-Chrabąszcz

Proofreader
Magdalena Jankosz

Typesetter
Katarzyna Mróz-Jaskuła

Jagiellonian University Press
Editorial Offices: Michałowskiego St. 9/2, 31-126 Kraków
Phone: +48 12 663 23 81, +48 12 663 23 82, Fax: +48 12 663 23 83